THE CROSS AND GREAT LIVING

THE CROSS
AND GREAT LIVING

By
William E. Phifer, Jr

ABINGDON-COKESBURY PRESS
New York • *Nashville*

THE CROSS AND GREAT LIVING
COPYRIGHT, MCMXLIII
By WHITMORE & STONE

SET UP, PRINTED, AND BOUND BY THE PARTHENON PRESS AT NASHVILLE, TENNESSEE, UNITED STATES OF AMERICA

TO

HER

WHO DAILY

SETS BEFORE THE AUTHOR

AN EXAMPLE OF

GREAT LIVING

PREFACE

THE SERMONS IN THIS VOLUME WERE ORIGINALLY preached to congregations of the Westminster Presbyterian Church of Nashville, Tennessee, during the tense days of the spring of 1942. Humbly they are offered to a larger audience with the earnest hope that the inherent truth of the cross may be illuminated somewhat. They are a simple attempt to throw across the pathway of our confused living some of the gleaming, white light that shines from the cross of Jesus Christ.

Naturally there is an abundance of literature on the subject. The cross is the focal point of all human history. Around it have clustered the hopes and desires of men and women in every age. It still remains the one hope of a distraught and weary world. But it is a hope that is sure, and those of us who have felt its power have no doubt that it shall yet be the sign in which we shall conquer.

It is to be expected that conditions change rapidly in the sort of world in which we find ourselves. But fundamental truth does not change. It is to the fundamentals that this book would address itself, while drawing largely for its material from present-day occurrences. Like the current of a stream, religious truth flows relentlessly onward through narrows, through shallows, through

7

rapids, through many changes of scenery. Truth is eternal, and at the heart of truth stands the cross of the Saviour.

If one burden is lightened, if one tear is dried, if one hope is quickened, if one life is changed, the volume will have served the purpose entertained by its author.

WILLIAM E. PHIFER, JR.

CONTENTS

9

THE CROSS AND HUMAN EXPERIENCE

But now in Christ Jesus ye who sometimes were far off are made nigh by the blood of Christ.—Eph. 2:13.

THERE IS A NEGRO SPIRITUAL WHICH GOES SOME-thing like this:

> Were you there when they crucified my Lord?
> . . . .
> Sometimes it causes me to tremble, tremble, tremble,
> Were you there when they crucified my Lord?

The words of that song bothered me no little for a time, because I could not see what meaning lay behind them. It is of no effect to sing words simply because they happen to fit a melody; unless there is some meaning behind the words there is no point to the whole effort. Suddenly it dawned on me that I had been too superficial in my attempts to discover the meaning. The song represented the heart of a burdened race; it sprang from the depths of being of a people who knew the ways of hardship and discouragement; it was the distilled essence of generations of religious meditation; it represented, in a way that I had not been able to express, the underlying identification of the cross of Christ with the moving currents of human experience. Here was the wording of a deeper understanding of the incarnation of Christ, and his supreme sacrifice, than many learned theologians had been able to phrase. Truly out of the mouths of babes shall come wisdom.

There is no more deep-rooted need of our world in the present era than such an identification of experience with the cross of the Master. We have observed the ethical content of his living, and have exclaimed in awe, "Such a way of life is too high for me; I cannot attain unto it!" We have studied the content of his teaching and have been amazed at the insight of the Man into the problems that have baffled the best minds of the ages. We have admired his idealisms, admitted his wisdom, laid hold upon his promises. But too often we have failed to realize that the deepest and most significant value of the life and work of Christ lies in the identification of his cross with the world, and more particularly with the individual. The death of this Man, in a way true of no other, is bound up with the history of the race, and with the life of each individual.

Yet who can put such thoughts into words? It is easy enough, in its way, to preach a sermon about the radiance of Christmas; it is quite a different matter to attempt to gather together the threads that compose the tragic events of the last week of the life of Jesus, and weave them into some suitable pattern. The facts are there, to be seen readily enough; but their meaning and their application somehow elude the feeble vehicles of expression we have. Milton wrote a poem on the birth of Jesus Christ, "On the Morning of Christ's Nativity." He had expected to write a companion piece on the death of the Master, but when he set himself to the task he found that he could not accomplish it. In the published works of the poet you will find the uncompleted beginning with a note attached to it which reads as follows: "This Subject the Author finding to be above the years he had when he wrote it, and nothing satisfied with what was begun, left it unfinished." We preachers all know that experience! The truths of the cross are so vast that they elude us. The facts of the passion of Christ are so close to each heart that we dare not attempt to express it all lest we discover ourselves in the midst of some confession more private than we care to share with others. The cross is the center of human experience; our desires and hopes cluster around its tragic consummation. The cross is at once a sign, an assertion, and a demand.

I

It is a sign that God does enter human living in every part of its whole. In the fact of the cross we have the assurance of a God who knows the depths of human degradation and suffering because he has been identified with it in actual experience. God has crossed the chasm which separates the divine from the human, and has become one with his children in every experience through which they pass. What a vast and adventurous thing that is when one considers it carefully! What a mighty and comforting thing it is when one looks out upon a world doomed to suffering and despair of every imaginable sort! God has not forgotten us in our difficulties because he can never forget the agony of the moments on the cross. The crucifixion is not an isolated event in human history; it is forever the sign that God is one with his people.

God has always been in action in the world. His providences have surrounded it, and his will has upheld it. By his word the swinging stars were fastened in their places, and day and night stalked majestically along the corridors of the heavens. Think of the daring adventure of creating a world and peopling it with human beings—with animals given the power to think and plan and choose. What faith in humanity that was to be the creation must have taken on the part of God! But in that action the adventure of God only began. His was the power that would continue perpetually the acts of providence that keep the planets in their appointed courses. His was the power that would influence the hearts of men to follow appointed paths of destiny. His was the power that would proclaim unto a wayward and sinful race of men the eternal truth of the authority of love. "Closer than breathing, and nearer than hands and feet," he was the power who would cause man to know that the world is not a place of terrible loneliness, but arched over by the sheltering wings of the Creator. But even that was not enough for the Adventurous God. He could not keep away from the suffering of mankind. He could not leave men with the tragedy of sin unsolved. He could not be content with guiding a life and avoiding an intimate contact with its personal sad and evil way. So the passion of Christ became reality, and the only begotten Son of God took a part in this experience of life with us. He, "being in the form of God, thought it not robbery to be equal with God: but made himself of no reputation, and took upon him the form of a servant, and was made in the likeness of men." There is no more profound statement in the annals of humanity. God is one with us.

The God who could and would do that is not apt to forget us in these stirring days of present world disaster. The war has come home to some of us with startling reality. The eternal sympathy and understanding on the part of the Master are facts that comfort and stablish the hearts of men in trying moments such as these. As there sweeps in upon us the thought which Francis Thompson expresses in his poem "The Hound of Heaven," that God never lets us go, and even though we make our bed in hell he relentlessly pursues us, we find

15

all arguments against God shattered and all explanations of the rationality of the world destroyed before the overwhelming actuality of faith. God is with us in human living—"who can be against us? He that spared not his own Son, but delivered him up for us all, how shall he not with him also freely give us all things?" This God never lets us go; he enters into the innermost recesses of our living; he takes part in every sorrow as well as every joy; he is the Being who makes religion a thing of glory to fill the earth with his praise.

We do not see him as he comes to us, but we see the cross and we know the reality of his suffering. We know that God can be touched with the feeling of our infirmities; and the knowledge of divine sympathy, based on experience, becomes something tender, wistful, infinitely lovely in our living. Like the tides in the sea, God is lifting humanity upon his shoulders. Like the law of gravitation, holding all things in their places, God draws us to himself. The cross is forever the sign that he is with us, and in the midst of our suffering he is suffering, in the midst of our difficulties he is pointing a solution; in the midst of our darkened days he is coming again and again with a torch of hope to light the way of the future. In chaos he is struggling to bring order; in darkness he is struggling to bring light; amid injustice he is struggling to bring justice; wherever man is, there God is— the cross is our eternal guarantee of that truth.

16

II

In the second place the cross of Christ enters human experience in a peculiar way with its assertion that humanity is worth dying for—at least God thought so! In our modern day with its continued preachments of hatred against one nation or another as the shifting winds of international policy may demand, it is refreshing to know that God has never entertained any doubt of the fact that the human race is worth saving, even if it costs as much as a crucifixion in order to accomplish it. It is not difficult to become cynical in times like this, and to lose one's faith in the inherent goodness of mankind. Looking across the world as we know it, witnessing the senseless destruction of human life, human treasures, human accomplishments, it seems at times a sacrilege to think that the race of men is worth any effort at salvation. To let the whole race be destroyed, and begin some process of life all over again on a different scale, seemingly is a much more plausible attitude to assume. Why try to do anything with people who in twenty-five hundred years have indulged themselves in twenty-five hundred and seventeen wars? Why try to do anything with a generation which has seen twenty-seven wars take place since the armistice of 1918? Now the whole world is at it again—what's the use? Humanity is not worth the effort.

But God did not feel that way. The cross is an assertion that men are worth while and that the temporary passions which rule them are capable of being controlled, and that the possibilities which are inherent within humankind so much outweigh the apparent evil that any cost is not too much to pay. That is the sort of thing that will ultimately keep some of us from losing faith in the possibility of a better tomorrow. There is little that is encouraging in the news of the day or the plans for the morrow. We must come to see that man himself has the possibilities for great living, and that God was willing to seal his belief in that statement with the life of his only begotten Son.

We can find the fact verified in modern living if we are willing to read discerningly and think without prejudice. There is evidence that the stars of human brotherhood and decency and understanding and sympathy have not been blotted out entirely by the clouds that have risen to sweep across the face of the heavens. It is true that humanity has sunk to a low depth, but for every sign that the spark of the divine is not yet dead we take courage for the future.

Before the Germans declared war on Greece, the Greeks made notable progress against the weak side of the Axis, Italy. As they advanced, almost without hindrance, they captured an Albanian stronghold with the well-nigh unpronounceable name of Argyrokastron. An American correspondent who happened to be with the Greek armies at the time tells a story that bears repeating.

He writes of seeing a Greek woman weeping bitterly as she went among the bodies of the young Italians lying in the streets. Some were sorely wounded; some were dying; some already had crossed the boundary we call death. As this Greek woman went from one boy to another, binding up their wounds, caring for them as best she could, as if they were not her enemies but her sons, the reporter heard her saying over and over again, "They're too young to die, too young to die." It became a solemn refrain, expressing in its own manner the depth of feeling on the part of this stranger.

She knew that far away Italian women had borne these sons, had nurtured them, and given them all the hope and care and toil and love that forever distinguishes the mother heart, and had wept bitter tears as they had marched away. Now these sons of those women were awkward blotches on a city street, a sacrifice to the insensate desires of men—and they had not a mother to care for them. All of this must have been in the heart of that Greek woman as she ministered to them, for mothers are mothers, and women are women the world over. As that woman cared for those boys she stood in a capacity representative of all the mothers in the world, overreaching every barrier that the selfishness of man erects, and seeing only the suffering of fellow human beings. In that is much of our hope. The lights have not gone out entirely, but we do need to be reminded at times that innately human

19

beings are the most valuable contribution that God made to the world. God thought that the race of men was worth dying for—he saw beyond the selfishness and greed and lust, that deep within the human heart there is something eternally fine and true and good. Let us not lose the vision in this modern day.

III

Yet again, we have here in the cross a demand that we meet life, with its failures, in the same spirit as did the strange Figure hanging upon the cross. Browning has a phrase in one of his poems, "The worst turns the best to the brave." How forever expressive of the deeper currents of human living! Those who are able to take life in their hands and mold it according to the necessities of the moment, not according to their own desires, are the men and the women who lay the solid foundations on which the happiness of unborn generations shall rest. The thing has happened so often in our lesser affairs of living. Whistler failed at West Point. He was deeply humiliated, but it was the best thing that could have happened to him. Bunyan was cast into Bedford jail but from the jail there came ringing into the years *Pilgrim's Progress*. Goldsmith was unable to pass the examination to be a hospital mate, and could get no clientele as a physician. But out of the humiliation of it all there came *The Vicar of Wakefield*. So illustrations might be multiplied of men and women who have caused the worst to turn the best because they were brave.

It must be kept in mind that sacrifice for the good of mankind is never made in vain. For the moment it may seem to be useless, there may seem to be no gleam of hope in all the darkened sky above, but beyond the murk and mist, beyond the heavens themselves, is the eternal affirmation of God that they who suffer for some just and honorable cause shall have their reward. As Jesus hung on the cross the birds ceased their singing; darkness fell over the face of the earth; his bloodstained face lifted toward heaven in a cry of despair, "My God, why hast thou forsaken me?" Jesus was alone at the turning point of history; his decision could make or mar the future of all humanity. He chose to suffer; and, lo! the generations of men who have followed have found in him not only the salvation which he purchased, but also the inspiration of unparalleled fortitude in bearing that which must be. The cross may be blacked out for the moment, but it does not disappear—it remains the hope of all tired and discouraged and despairing men, for it shows to what uses a cross may be turned.

Pierre van Paassen puts it in a striking form in his recent book *That Day Alone.*

The river [of history] moves on, but the Cross remains, now as a vague vision that recedes in the night, then moving forward in stark reality. When the strong torture the weak, when the poor cry for bread, when the innocent languish in dungeons, when mothers go insane because they see their children die, when the outcasts roam in the wilderness, when the soldiers go to battle, when those who sit in darkness pray for light, the Cross returns, and the head of the Man on the Cross sinks deeper on the tired breast.[1]

Ultimately the whole matter becomes simply one of faith. Simply? There is nothing more profound than the faith of which I am speaking! When one attempts to break it into component parts it is not at all the sort of thing that will lend itself to such a process. It is a simple affirmation—God lives, and all is well. Some say it is a Pollyanna method of accepting that which is beyond our control, but such criticism is superficial. In our living there are some things that are indispensable to us if we are to retain our garments as men. Pain and disaster are a part of the sensitivity of the race, and without this sensitivity all creative ability would be destroyed. Music, art, poetry, all issue from the womb of sensitivity, and as this capacity to feel grows upon us, also does the capacity to suffer grow with it. The only possible way that we are able to bear with it all and win through to a satisfactory conclusion is to know "whom we have believed, and be persuaded that he is able to keep that which we have committed unto him."

[1] Dial Press, 1941, p. 537.

It is to such a crusade that I call you today. There will be moments when the knife is twisted in the breast and we will cry with Jesus, "O God, why have you forsaken me?" But for everyone who can hold fast to the vision of the cross there will come moments of calm understanding. Life is not an easy road, but the One with whom we have to do has been all the way before us. He enters into a fellowship with us in a way of which we would not have dared to dream had he not shown us its eternal truth. In that moving portrayal of the idea of God held by so many of the Negro race, as it was shown in the play *The Green Pastures*, there was one phrase which remained with me long after other memories of the play had faded away. I have reminded myself of it numbers of times—it helps tremendously when one feels that the universe is crashing about one's head. Do you remember the character called "de Lawd" as he said, "Even bein' Gawd ain't a bed of roses." If God must struggle, so must we; if his heart aches at times, can we expect that we shall go free?

In the cross of Christ we have a symbol to remind us that, if we will have it so, there is a power that can surmount evil, that can rise above tragedy, and carry off a victory in spite of all appearances. There is no other way! The hope of humanity lies in men learning to sing with the heart:

> In the cross of Christ I glory,
> Towering o'er the wrecks of time.

23

THE CROSS AND HUMAN VALUES

[Jesus] for the joy that was set before him endured the cross.—Heb. 12:2.

THE MOST TRAGIC EVENT THAT CAN OCCUR IN THE spiritual realm of a man's life is a confusion of the values of human experience. Yet how often has this thing happened to our neighbors and friends, and even to ourselves! In a day when the world is upset, its economy out of balance, its hours of suffering far outweighing its moments of happiness, each of us is prone to accept as dismal failures many of the maxims that we once trusted to redeem the world. We have been taught to believe that certain unseen forces are powerful, but today their power seems null and void as across the face of the earth the four horsemen of the Apocalypse ride their ghostly steeds, with nought to stay their progress. Our whole scheme of things is disrupted because of hatreds and misunderstandings between nations, and we are prone to discard certain values that a few years ago we would have guaranteed.

In making such an admission we must attempt at the same time to find some reasonable explanation for the fact, or we have confessed that the church has failed miserably in its mission. For we do not well to evade the issue: men today are doubtful if religion has the power to save the world as it has claimed for twenty centuries. Men are skeptical in regard to the entire process that Christianity offers, and they are not sure that the values offered in our religious experience are the sort that can promote happiness and bring in an era of peace and concord. Men are seeking an experimental morality, with little more than a utilitarian ethical content, hoping through this to discover some gleam of truth.

In order to win through to a satisfactory understanding of the deeper truths that are involved in this problem it is necessary to recognize the fact that there are two types of values in the world. The one type is capable of evolutionary development, and becomes more meaningful with the passing centuries. Of such are many of the material values that we know, each generation building upon the work of its predecessor. We cannot understand these values entirely by their present-day applications or uses, neither can we trace them ultimately to their origins. We do not explain a Gershwin tune by the beat of some tom-tom by half-naked savages, although we cannot escape the fact that the former grew out of the latter. We do not explain an intricate surgical process by the application of poultices of roots and berries to some aching abdomen, but we know that the one actually came from the other. There are values in life which are constantly fluctuating. That which is helpful to one generation is of no use to the next, and so the chain is lengthened, one link at a time.

But just as surely there are values that do not change with the passing years. Morality is not an experimental part of living, for its principles are abiding. Material things still are worth so much to us as food or shelter or clothing—only the outward form changes. In spite of necessities forced upon us by the rapidity of modern events, we know that some things abide forever. To lose this confidence is to give way to uncontrolled pessimism for the future. That is beyond the bounds of a Christian's reasoning. Perhaps in no area can the importance of the cross of Christ be more readily understood and accepted than in its proclamation of the eternity of certain values in life. That they are unseen does not lessen their power nor destroy their promise. Let me suggest three of these values to you in three words, love, service, redemption.

I

The first of these values that the cross illustrates is the fact that love is a power with which we must reckon. This sort of statement has been made with astonishing frequency when one considers the ignorance of it that seemingly abounds on every hand. Men have heard it said until no longer do they give it proper heed. But men have not connected the power of love with the affairs of everyday. It

26

is supposed to be some remote virtue to be manifested in the home or among a selected group of friends, but care must be exercised that it spread not too far afield. Consequently the very bases of our religious affirmations have come to be vitiated by the fact that men give lip service to them, but will not admit their actuality. Professor John Dewey has some grounds for his statement, "Nowhere in the world at any time has religion been so thoroughly respectable as with us and so nearly totally disconnected with life." [1]

We have so long associated with the respectability of religion that we have come to think carelessly and lightly of its fundamental tenets. Religion and Western culture have come to be synonymous in our mental attitudes. We have not taken the necessary thought and effort to realize that the two are not at all one and the same, though much that is good in our Western civilization has developed from the religion of Christ. Now, when the vaunted benefits of our culture are not only threatened but are rapidly disappearing, we need to remind ourselves that love can still manifest its power, no matter what happens to everything else. Love showed its strength there on the cross; love has not changed in its abiding reality. The foundations of the old order are already gone. As we start to build for the future let it not be forgotten

[1] Quoted in Justin Wroe Nixon, *The Moral Crisis in Christianity*, Harper & Bros., 1931, p. 78.

that the power which overthrew the Roman Empire
in less than four hundred years was love, as shown
by a helpless Man hanging on a cross.

It all sounds rather silly in a day when we are
gathering together the might that we possess in
order to go out and destroy as much and as many
as possible. But we Christians can still hold fast
to the ultimacy of the good, even though for the
moment we are forced into something beyond our
control. We have no underlying hatreds for those
with whom we are at war. Every opportunity will
be afforded us to prove that such is the case. We
do not hear our leaders urging us, as Mussolini
did some time ago, "to develop a hate that is cold,
conscious, implacable, a hate in every home, that
is indispensable for victory."

For the moment it is necessary that we take arms
against forces of evil that our race has developed.
We have no right to assume that we are without
sin in the matter, or that we have no responsibility
for a world such as this one. We are all part of
the fabric, and as such we have obligations. We
make no attempt to justify the war from the stand-
point of our personal righteousness. Had we been
all that we should have been in the community of
nations, it might not have happened. But now
that it is here we must see to it that the principles
of right and justice triumph.

However, the most important matter with which
we have to do is the maintenance in our own hearts

28

of a spirit of understanding. We must keep alive the fact that love is a powerful weapon, and that even though we may be forced to administer chastisement of a horrible sort upon those who would destroy us, we still love them as children of God and brothers in Christ. Then when the war stops we shall be ready to do our part in the building of a world where this sort of thing does not occur periodically. A man who fell from the roof of a house was asked by a neighbor if the fall hurt him. "No," said the man, "the fall didn't hurt me. It was the stopping that nearly killed me." Let us see to it that the stopping of this war is not worse that its prosecution. Let us maintain in our consciousness the guarantee given us by the cross that love is a mighty power, and that through love we may build a world that no other power could ever establish.

II

The second value that the cross proclaims to have an eternal significance is one stated by Jesus himself: "Whosoever will save his life shall lose it." It looks and sounds like a crazy upheaval of everything that the world would teach us. It appears utterly paradoxical that a man should save his life by losing it, should redeem it by throwing it away. Certainly it does not sound like the practical common sense that all of us would like to claim as a part of our living.

Yet the facts of life are such that the truth of the statement is verified time and again. Those who have given away some treasure have discovered that it came back to them fourfold. Those who have sacrificed some heart's desire have discovered that their lives were more than filled with a compensatory happiness. Those who have lost their lives have found that they have just begun to live, and that the intensity of human experience depends upon our renunciation of that intensity. Jesus hanging upon the cross was the forerunner of a great body of men and women who have been willing to suffer the slings and arrows of outrageous fortune willingly, quietly, hopefully, knowing that their reward would not be withheld.

Recently I came across a story arising out of World War days which is a forceful illustration of the idea. A company of Negro soldiers were in the camp at Fort Dodge, Iowa. A group of them was selected for officers' school and sent to Arkansas to receive that training. Upon arrival they were met with a rather cool reception, and the first time they were lined up for instruction the white officer assigned to them spoke in bitter tones: "This thing has been forced upon me. I didn't join the army to train a gang of niggers. So long as I am your commanding officer you will work fifteen hours a day, and if you get commissions it will be in spite of me."

When the men were dismissed they were ripe

30

for a race riot. Some wanted to waylay the officer and beat him up. Some wanted to run amuck through the entire camp as long as they were able to get away with it. Some wanted to desert the army and throw up the whole thing.

Finally a quiet little man secured the attention of the group and spoke to them: "Listen, fellows. We are Negroes, but we are also American soldiers. We represent the best that our race affords or we wouldn't have been selected for this special training. Our honor is at stake, and the eyes of America are upon us. Let's play the game, and be as square as we can about it, and trust in God." His counsel prevailed, and the men agreed to do as he suggested.

No group of soldiers ever worked harder than this company of Negroes. Their rifles were never clean enough; their clothes were never neat enough; their marching was never done. Oftentimes they were required to stand at attention for an hour or more on some pretext or other. And constantly they were abused and cursed and berated in every possible manner. But toward the end of the course the white officer in charge seemed to relent a little, and when the examinations were over 55 per cent had passed and received their commissions as lieutenants in the army—a very creditable percentage of the whole.

A near-by city found its colored population giving a farewell dance for the successful contestants on the night the school closed. Oddly enough the white officer was present, and he asked to make a statement. He explained that his attitude toward the Negro race was occasioned by the fact that his father, who had been a sheriff in Oklahoma, had been killed by Negro bandits. From the day of his father's death he had vowed that he would avenge that murder in every way possible upon the whole race of Negro people. He had become known far and wide for the intensity of his feeling against them, and when he had been assigned the duty of training a company of colored soldiers he had welcomed it as an opportunity to wreak further displeasure upon a group over which he had complete authority. But they had beaten him at his game! They had seen, through the leadership of one man of insight, that the only way to gain life was to lose it. So they had submitted to the punishment; and now, on the night of the graduation, here was the white officer, with tears in his eyes, saying, "I'm proud of this company. I love every man in it. And I'm your friend until I die."

Passing by the problem of race relations that may be involved, is there not a message for each of us in that sort of solution of a difficulty? The church certainly can take its place in a hard and cruel world to declare with unhesitating reality that the man who wishes to save his life must lose it. So long as the voice of the Christian church does ring out with no uncertain note, we may be well assured that the future of the world is safeguarded. For some will heed that voice and, looking back across the centuries, will see once more the figure of One who was stretched agonizingly upon the outreaching arms of a Roman cross, saying, "Father, forgive them"; and those few who catch the deepest significance of that sentence will redeem the world.

III

This is the third of the values that the cross declares is eternal: the possibilities of man's redemption. In another sermon in this volume we have spoken of the fact that the cross affirms for us that God believed that man was *worth dying for*. Now we assert that the cross reminds us that man is *capable* of being redeemed. Of course there would be no point in dying for that which is worthless; there would be no meaning to the sacrifice of the Master unless man were capable of being restored to a place of close fellowship with God. The fact that Jesus died is a constant reminder that we can come close to our Creator when the desire stirs strong enough within our breasts.

We have been associated with the brute side of man's nature for so long, and in so intimate a manner, that we have sometimes forgotten that the spirit of man is not limited, but may rise with the wings of the eagle to soar to the sun. We have been reminded so often of the hatreds that stir men's hearts that we have forgotten that man can love so deeply and so earnestly that life itself is changed from monotonous rhythm to melodies of paradise. We have seen so much sin and suffering and sorrow that we have forgotten that "they that wait upon the Lord shall renew their strength; they shall mount up with wings as eagles; they shall run, and not be weary; and they shall walk, and not faint." Frankwood E. Williams, in his volume *Adolescence*, has a striking statement:

We can conceive of a body of men and women able to deal intellectually with reality, who will see and deal with things as they are . . . . men and women capable of living rich emotional lives, but this life growing out of the joy of life itself as it becomes aware of the infinite emotional wealth of the world itself; a life lived from within, but in relation to the world about; not a life chaotic within through anxiety and fear, swinging with every wind, running precipitately to shelter, fighting windmills; but a life secure within, not through the repression or denial of fear and anxiety, but in which these simply do not exist, or exist as little as is humanly possible, so minimized as not to be determinants in personality, character and conduct. . . . . There are individuals whose lives are secure in this sense . . . . capable of being loved generously, because capable of loving generously.[2]

That is the sort of philosophy of which the

[2] Pp. 84-85. Copyright, 1930, by Frankwood E. Williams, and reprinted by permission of Farrar & Rinehart, Inc., publishers.

world has dire need today. We have allowed ourselves the doubtful advantage of speculation in
regard to the future, and that which we see there
in our crystal-gazing manner is not as pleasant as
we should like it to be. What has happened to
our race is awful to contemplate. We are disturbed, distressed, worried, anxious over it all.
Then comes the reassuring picture of the cross of
Christ. There on either side of the gentle Nazarene
was a hardened criminal, and from each of them
there came the selfish cries which characterized
their whole living: "Why don't you do something?
If you are God, why do we have to suffer like
this?" And then something happened to one of
those men. He had a vision of something he had
not understood before. He saw truth gleaming in
the sky, and he turned his face upward that its
beams might fall full upon him. Crying to his
friend to cease his blasphemy he said, "We are
suffering the just penalties for our misdeeds, but
this man has done nothing amiss. Lord, remember
me when thou comest into thy kingdom." And
Jesus promised that nothing should keep him from
paradise.

All of that sounds strangely modern to us!
Men on every hand are asking, "Why doesn't God
do something?" little realizing that God is suffering
just as much as his wayward children. But here
and there those who have an insight not granted
to all of us are lifting their faces toward heaven and

crying, "We know, O God, that we are suffering the just deserts of our deeds. But have mercy upon us, and for thy name's sake pardon our iniquities, and bring us into thine everlasting kingdom." And every time that sort of voice is raised in petition toward heaven there is an answer—a still small voice speaks with comforting words of peace, and the restless soul finds its haven.

The Pope in Browning's *The Ring and the Book* tells of a certain night in Naples, so dark that one could scarcely have guessed that anywhere about was earth or sky or sea or world at all. "But the night's black was burst through by a blaze." One flash of lightning had revealed the surrounding mountains, the city of thick population, and the sea stretching into infinite night. "So," he says, "may the truth be flashed out by one blow." In one instant a man may see that of which he had not dreamed and the currents of his existence may be changed thereby.

All in all, we cannot escape the fact that the cross of Christ does have a tremendous significance in the life of each one of us. Standing like a signal light upon some peak of time, it illumines for us each of the darkened ways that we must tread. Here is not an isolated historical event, but one which is woven into the fabric of living in such a manner that never shall we escape its compelling power. The cross is not only our hope; it is our inspiration. It calms and soothes the chaotic wastes of lives dedicated to no high purposes. In the dim gray leagues that lie ahead for each of us we see a gleaming star, and the warmth of that star penetrates the icy breaths which blow upon us, and we are no longer afraid or worried or concerned. Life is good, and God is kind, and Christ is real—we shall yet build a new world.

THE CROSS AND GREAT
LIVING

Christ also suffered for us, leaving us an example,
that ye should follow his steps.—I Pet. 2:21.

GREAT EPOCHS IN HUMAN HISTORY HAVE BEEN, IN
large measure, those which were controlled by
great dreams. Men who have reached out beyond
the seen and begun to deal with eternal, unseen
realities of the spirit have been the ones who have
kindled the imagination of their fellows and pointed
for humanity the road to fuller and richer existence.
Through the co-ordination of every power for
good, and the binding of it all together with a
vision of the possibilities inherent in the human race,
men have come to discover new avenues of service
and personal happiness. Some great adventure of
the spirit has called, and men have answered because they have felt the moving power of an inner
urge born of their dream of the future.

Oftentimes these observations become actuality
through the impact of a great personality. Men
discuss avidly some renovation of the methods of
life, but they wait for some leader to show them
the way of accomplishment. Then, captivated by
his energies and his undying confidence in the
dream that possesses him, they are willing to follow

his guidance into the promised land. That his energies are misplaced and his dream is decadent is often the misfortune of the world. What marvelous sources of good might be tapped if the spirit which controls Hitler or Mussolini were of a different nature! They are men who have unwavering confidence in themselves and their mission; they are men who have used the power of dreaming more than those of lesser caliber round about them. The strength of their dreaming is witnessed by enslaved nations all over the world. That it has been largely evil does not lessen the fact of its power.

Therefore, those who are planning a world of tomorrow, in which happiness and not despair shall rule, must be always careful of the type of dreaming in which they indulge. If a man is to be successful in great living he must be sure that his imagination is kindled and his energies harnessed in a search for the best. That this is not an easy task is readily admitted, but its possibilities are the hopes that make our world livable. As men we know what we might be, and at times we are stirred within our hearts to attempt to reach such a goal.

In no part of life is the compelling nature of the cross of Christ more apparent than here. It has been said that no one yet has lived or died in the spirit of the Master without someone else catching this Divine Spirit and entering into a fullness of life. Jesus had a vision of that which mankind could be, and he sealed his belief in the reality of that vision with his own blood. That sacrifice remains for the centuries an unparalleled example of the way in which great living is attained.

I

Here we are shown the real way to meet a difficult situation. A modern writer points out that the first question that ought to be asked by any group or any individual facing a hazardous situation is whether or not the crisis is to be met as a challenge or an occasion for despair. The attitude in which we accept such moments of unusual stress is not only indicative of the quality of nobility which we may possess; it is a foundation stone for future living. If we fail in moments of extreme hardship, we have forfeited our right to a place in the advance of humanity. The difficulties that beset our living may be used as stepping stones to higher and nobler accomplishments, even though the course we are following necessarily may be reset. To be able to accept that which comes into our lives in such a manner that even the evil contributes to some good end is to find the deepest secret of human nobility. Because Jesus knew that secret he died upon a cross.

A number of years ago a young Englishman named Henry Fawcett was hunting with his father. The older man, shooting at a bird, hit his son's eyes and blinded him completely. Writing about the matter sometime later, young Fawcett said, "I made up my mind within ten minutes after the accident to stick to my main purpose so far as in me lay." He kept his word, worked his way through Cambridge University, was made professor of political economy there, and later became post-master-general of England, devising for the British people the system of parcel post which we in America adopted a generation later. Fawcett met the situation facing him in the manner that great living always meets these things. He was surrounded by despair, but was not overcome by it. He was shrouded in disappointment, but was not over-whelmed by it. He saw that the thing which had happened to him was something about which he could do nothing. Therefore he resolved to use it and not be abused by it.

That fine phrase of Matthew Arnold's concerning his friend, "who saw life steadily and saw it whole," has its essential place in all of our thinking. Because one disaster befalls us let it not be thought that this marks the end of all things. Jesus did not feel that way about the cross which he carried up the hill to Golgotha. Certainly no worse catastrophe could have happened to him. Yet he was willing to accept that cross, and the death it entailed, because he was assured that for righteousness and justice there is no death, no matter how apparent may be their decease to a materialistic world.

41

We too must keep that thought uppermost if we are adequately to evaluate the situations that face us.

To many people it seems that all the things for which they have labored have failed. In our day we have witnessed the destruction of many values we thought were permanent, the breakdown of many ideals we had counted upon to save us from despair. Immediately after the Paris Conference, at the close of the last war, Lloyd George remarked, "That conference will settle the destiny of nations and the course of human life for God knows how many ages." But it did not settle them even for one generation! Such tragic realities cannot fail to make indelible impressions upon some hearts that had committed themselves to the good, the true, the beautiful. Moments of complete cynicism have swept the spirits of some, and the expression, "What's the use?" has come into popularity.

Undoubtedly, the thing we need most in such a bewildering age is a proper approach to the solution of the matter. We have ranged over the fields of science and economics and politics, and, with their aid, attempted to work out plausible solutions of our difficulties. It is high time we realized that these things do not work without a proper undergirding, and that we have neglected to provide the spiritual basis upon which alone they could operate successfully. We must not forget that we are human beings, with grave responsibilities for the sort of world in which we live. Since many of

42

the untoward facts of our lives are of our own making, let us face them resolutely and find a way out. It is possible, when we are ready to give ourselves to the venture unreservedly. Certainly, such was the Jesus way.

II

But there are always those critics who would attempt to destroy our faith by saying that religion is a Utopian dream, utterly incapable of practical realization. Religion, they say, is an opiate which robs the people of virility by its soothing-syrup doctrines of love and good will. But they have not made out their case. Religion, in its truest form, is not nearly so romantic and soft as our popular rendition of it has made it appear. We have extracted the sweetness and ignored the profound, and sometimes terrifying, realism that is there. Jesus was not taken in by such shallow views. He faced up to all the terrible facts of his existence just as they were, and met them courageously and hopefully. The secret of great living is hidden in such abilities.

Religion, as an objective reality in human experience, has certain facts which are its mainstay. These facts must become part of our spiritual equipment if we are to discover a way of life similar to that which Jesus followed. This means that we must come to see, just as Jesus clearly and constantly saw, that life has no reality apart from

43

its spiritual heritage. Philosophers may write their learned treatises; scholars may send forth vaporistic theorizing; but when all is said and done you and I must face the exigencies of everyday, somehow. Here are pressing problems that we cannot escape, and theories and complex analyses heaped in upon us do not solve them for us. There must come the assurance that faith and hope and love do count, and that the material things with which we are surrounded have weight only as we allow it to be so.

In short, life must be undergirded by the spiritual, or great living is impossible. Jesus hanging upon the cross had nothing left but his faith—his unquenchable belief that the hand of God was in this matter, and therefore the issues would be safeguarded. The material too often proves a weak reed, and we find that the support we so desperately need at times is totally lacking. Seemingly, material things offer all that is necessary; but when a testing time comes, only he who has the power of the spirit is able to continue. The story goes that Sir Christopher Wren ran out of money near the end of the building of St. Paul's Cathedral in London. So he found it necessary to make the massive columns mere shells, filled with waste and rubbish. They were imposing looking, seemingly solid enough to last for centuries, but time told the story. The walls began to crack and the dome tilted and the sham was exposed. The incident is a parable that needs no elucidation.

44

Someone well points out that we do not lack in faith—we lack simply in faith in the right sort of things. We rush about with fanatic zeal, ready to believe everything that is told us. Our faith in the things we hear amounts to actual credulity at times. Especially if the item is of a juicy scandalous nature are we ready to accept it at its face value, with no questions asked. With frenzied fury we accept the dicta of horoscopes, crystal-gazers, fortunetellers, and so on through a maze of money and power and social prestige. We all misplace a great deal of our faith.

A similar statement might be made in regard to our hope. We look across the years to come and have hopes for many things, but in themselves they are often groundless because based on false premises. We cannot reasonably expect their fulfillment, for they have no permanent foundation upon which to rest.

Consider the third of the eternal virtues, love. We have sufficient love but we do not direct its channels aright. On what things are our affections fixed most ardently? Those things that lift us, or those that prove weights upon our spiritual progress? It is perfectly possible to love those things and those people who will lift us from the ordinary affairs of everyday and cause us to tread the paths that lead between the stars. But we must make the choice between that sort of love and the baseless, senseless kind that destroys much of the finer sensibilities of living. Ruskin wisely remarks: "The closest, deepest, trial question of the human heart is simply, what do you like? Tell me what you truly like, what are your deepest satisfactions, and I will tell you what you are."

Some of us have made the vital mistake of putting all of our faith and hope and love in the ephemeral things of the world. We have loved wealth, and security, and ease, getting our deepest satisfaction in life from things that we touch and call our own. Then there come trying days such as these, in which it seems that the world is cracking up, and the things in which we believed are in dire danger of disappearing. What happens to those who have no spiritual resources with which to meet the situation?

Dr. Henry Hitt Crane tells of receiving in his mail one morning a letter which provided a clue for much understanding about life and its problems. It came from the son of one of his best friends. The friend had died suddenly in a Western hotel, and the letter was a request of Dr. Crane that he conduct the funeral services. The man had been a grand person, pioneer in religious education, superb teacher, master of practical details, yet ever visionary, an able administrator, and a magnificent Christian. Yet he had been totally misunderstood by his colleagues, and because of their petty jealousies had been subjected to a series of tests that would have broken the spirit of a lesser man. He did break once, but then he rallied, and wrote a book summing up his convictions and the lessons of his hard experience. Yet in all that book there was not a line of malice, no hint of bitterness, resentment, or desire for revenge on those who had misused him. It was a swan song of pure spiritual triumph. And now he was dead! One part of the letter from the young man was particularly impressive.

Doubtless you are aware of the keynote of my father's life, the secret of his amazing courage, power and faith. I think it is best expressed by his favorite little verse—a copy of which I found in his pocket-book. It's a translation of something by Victor Hugo, I believe:

> "On a branch that swings
> Sits a bird that sings—
> Knowing that he has wings!" [1]

There is the answer for which many of us have been seeking. He who knows that he has wings has a song in his life, and is not afraid of the storms that sweep through the forest. What if the branch does break? He has wings, and the reality of that fact gives him assurance and weaves itself into the melody of his lilting song. So, they who seek the Lord with their whole heart are not afraid. They know Whom they have believed, and they have a song, knowing they have wings.

[1] *The Christian Century Pulpit*, September, 1941, p. 196.

III

There is a further thing that ought to be mentioned. The cross is for us that tangible something that so often we need to bolster our failing faith. At moments when the sun is sinking behind some cloud of disappointment or despair or grief, our hearts are aghast at the frightfulness of the experience, and we are tempted to accept the advice of Job's wife and "curse God, and die." The cross proves its deepest worth at such times, for we are reminded by it that this Man passed through similar experiences. At the cross we are not asked to face uncertain futures, we are not asked to speculate as to ways of escape—here is reality, as hard and crushing as any with which we have to deal. Here is something the very historicity of which guarantees its truth. Whatever one may think of the cross as a redemptive factor, its example must be allowed. Here is tangible truth on which we may lay firm hold, no matter what else may be swept from under us.

From such realization there comes the conviction that we are all partners in this bold venture of God's. This idea of saving a human race is no small conception. Unaided we could not have come into such knowledge, for it defies the limitations of our intelligence. But with God we understand it, for there upon the cross hangs his only begotten Son, to make it plain that this is no imaginary gospel, but the most real event that ever swam into the consciousness of mankind. This thinking produces for us the faith that is necessary to play our part well.

In this cosmic adventure of redemption each person has a share. Some have been granted ten talents, and some much less, but all are necessary to the whole. It may be that your part is the bearing of a daily cross with fortitude, so that others, seeing, may take heart for the future. It may be that your part is to enter some arena to destroy some wild beast of public dishonor. It may be that your part is to make the welkin ring with the proclamation of the "good news." Whatever it may be, the world will not be as good a place as it might be if you fail in the consummate giving of yourself to the venture.

This will require that you have faith in the venture itself. Whenever men lose faith in the worth of the enterprise in which they are engaged their energies subside and their morale declines. Winston Churchill illustrates this truth in an account of his visit to General Haig's headquarters in August, 1918, when the general was ordering an attack by three British armies on the German line north and south of Bapaume. Indicating on the map the Wotan, the Brunhilde, the Siegfried, and the Hindenburg lines, perhaps the most superb defenses erected by any army during the war, General Haig said to Churchill, "Now you will see what these fortifications are worth when troops are no longer resolved to defend them." [2]   The sequel proved that Haig was right. The fortifications, the guns, the physical equipment, the troops, were all there. But something was lacking, and that something proved the undoing of the German plans. Men must believe or there is no possibility of success.

It is not easy to follow Jesus in a world like this. An abiding, sustaining, realistic experience of the cross is more earnestly needed than any other thing by modern Christians. Someday we shall come to see that this is the only practical way of life that has ever been devised. For those who catch the vision there can begin at the moment great and noble living.

[2] Winston Churchill, *The World Crisis, 1916-18,* Charles Scribner's Sons, 1927, II, 248.

THE CROSS AND DUTY

For this cause came I unto this hour.—John 12:27.

AN ANALYSIS OF THE MOTIVES THAT LED THE LORD Jesus to the cross would be incomplete did it ignore the fact that Jesus suffered the crucifixion partly because he conceived it to be his duty. He was so devoted to the ideal of what he ought to do that he did not count the cost. His whole life was so given over to the rounding out of a character in accord with the character of God that he derived his highest pleasure in doing the things that ought to be done, not in following the devices of his own ways. Certainly love motivated his acceptance of the cross; but we do not well to ignore the feeling that prompted him to say, "For this cause came I unto this hour." He conceived it to be his duty to suffer, and duty was one of the foundation stones on which he built his life.

What is this strange stirring within a man's breast that we call duty? Haeckel says that duty is "a long series of phyletic modifications of the phronema of the cortex." I suppose this means that duty is simply a physical movement of the outer layer of the brain. Of course, this is begging the question in a sense, for the movements themselves

THE CROSS AND GREAT LIVING

are still unexplained. Wordsworth, the poet, says
that duty is the "Stern Daughter of the Voice of
God." He intimates that God speaks to man
through this sense of obligation that is inherent in
the souls of all of us.

Much of the modern scientific research apparently is bearing out the claims of Haeckel. The
chemist has come to the rescue of a modified be-
havioristic attitude toward life, and has confidently
assured us that character and disposition are largely
determined by chemical reactions within the body.
One scientist is quoted as saying:

> The chemist of the future will turn from the humble
> task of providing the conveniences of life and gain
> control of life itself. He may mould stature and
> character as the sculptor moulds his clay. . . . . Courage
> is not a matter of "sand" but of sugar. A variation
> of a few hundredths of one per cent of glucose in the
> blood may make the difference between courage and
> cowardice; may determine whether a man be shot as a
> slacker or medalled as a hero.[1]

Definitions of the concept of duty are woefully
inadequate. We have no disposition to accept with
unquestioning credulity the dicta of the scientists.
It seems unthinkable that sugar in the blood could
have sent Jesus to the cross. Nor can we bear
with the behaviorist who says that a spasm of the
brain will make a man dutiful or not. We must

[1] Quoted in John F. Troupe, *Interviewing God*, Fleming H.
Revell Co., 1930, p. 73.

blaze our own trail if we are properly to understand the phenomenon in man's living that enables
him to say, "This is my duty. I will do the thing
in this manner."

I

First, we note that all the data that the centuries
have contributed to our knowledge of duty con-
firm the fact that duty is the interpreter of true
human living. Man, as a spiritual being, reaches up
for that which is beyond his grasp. Consciously he
exerts his will to outlive his primitive and imperfect
state. Continually he sets up idealisms and struggles toward them, even though they be centuries
in fulfillment. Man is an animal who seeks and
penetrates and discerns, and having found a path
that he wishes to follow because of a promised
reward he is willing to travel that road regardless
of the stones that hinder his progress. The cross
of the Christ is the supreme example of this sort
of living. Jesus, "for the joy that was set before
him, endured the cross, despising the shame."
Through an unalterable devotion to the plainly
marked path of duty he found strength to climb
the hill on which a cross was set.

Man's superiority in the world does not consist
in his physical importance. Man is not as fleet as
a deer, nor as strong as a horse, nor as big as an
elephant. His vision is not as keen as the eagle's;
his sense of smell is not as highly developed as that

of a dog; he does not grow his own clothing as does the sheep. In many ways animals far surpass their distant cousin. But in the realm of the spirit there is no comparison, for into that realm the animal does not enter. The elevation of man consists in the co-ordination he is able to make between his heart and his will. Selecting a course of living, he is able to continue therein because it is his duty, and that intangible something is enough to keep him there. The urge to comfort and convenience is forgotten in the trumpeting of duty's demands.

If the interpretation of life is to be discovered through duty, it follows that man must find some cause which is big enough to make demands upon him. No petty crusade can call forth the hidden possibilities of a man. There must be wholehearted allegiance to something outside oneself, and much bigger than oneself. Jesus could not have died for small reasons. Negatives could not have set his soul aflame with passion for righteousness. He was immersed in his belief in the necessity of his atoning death, and so firmly did he believe that the crucifixion was his appointed destiny that he was willing to forsake all else and bear it.

Tragically, this generation found itself without a cause in which to believe. The first World War brought more clouds than it dispelled, and out of the gloom nothing worth while emerged for youth to hold fast. In certain parts of the world shrewd demagogues recognized this plastic moment in history, and offered a program and a cause to youth. They seized it avidly, and through the streets of Berlin and Rome and Moscow hundreds of thousands of young men and women marched with banners aloft to proclaim to the world that the millennium was at the door, waiting to be ushered in. "We will build a new empire," sang the Fascist. "We are remaking the world," chanted the Communist. "We are building a greater Germany," proclaimed the Nazi. Pathetically they waved their flags and shouted their slogans, while their leaders were plotting a course that would leave these same enthusiastic youngsters strewn like offal across the battlefields of the world. They had found a cause, but it was not the right sort, and the fountains of blood that are issuing throughout our world today are tragic witness to the inadequacy of such conceptions of duty as motivate these young people.

In our own land there has been too often on the part of the young people a lassitude toward life that has produced sorrowful results. In America the favorite words of recent years have been "Security," "Pensions," "Thirty dollars every Thursday," "Ham and eggs every day," and other economic nonsense. Young people are not stirred by such ideas. Their sense of duty is not prodded by such goads. Consequently they have become like the young man in one of May Sinclair's novels— perfectly content to lie in a swinging hammock, sipping iced drinks, while someone else produces the music that sweetens the moments. Life has no abiding meaning until some cause lays hold upon us! But once it grips us, devotion to it, loyalty to its principles, unswerving obedience to its demands, make of human life a thing of beauty forever. Duty is the password that opens these doors to all who would go in. Discover the cause; conceive it to be your duty to follow it; and the devils in hell will tremble before you.

II

In the second place we find that duty is many times the true interpreter of human powers. It may be a disillusioning thought, but it is pre-eminently true, that most of us never live up to our full capacities. Human-like, we must be prodded and goaded into the accomplishments we are able to number. John Knox once remarked, "The world is still waiting to see what God can do with a man wholly consecrated to his service." Such a thought is applicable to all of living. If any one of us did all the things that we could do, the scheme of living would be considerably altered.

But a crisis provides an outlet for much pent-up energy, and is the sound in the tops of the mulberry trees that summons men to battle. Duty is the call for which men are waiting, and it is gloriously true in the history of the race that men are ready to answer that call when it comes. It may be that such does not appear to be the highest motive possible, but who is able to say what value a motive has in the ultimate analysis of life? So long as man does rise to meet the emergency that confronts him, we have no right to assume that he is less a man because it was an emergency that called forth his latent powers. Jesus met the cross, not with stoic resignation, but with full appreciation of all that was involved in the plan of God for him and the world. He met it because he conceived it to be his duty, and we have no right to say that such a motive is not the very highest of all.

Certainly we have discovered that life offers us opportunities to measure up to that which duty whispers. Whenever we answer that whisper confidently, we feel an added strength given to our wavering wills. William James suggests for us that there are whole strata of our living in which the energies and the possibilities have not been touched. It is the province of each individual to seek out these areas and bring their treasures to the front. Professor James believed that every man can double his present capacities for accomplishment if he is willing to make the effort. He tells of men dying of thirst in the desert, falling prostrate in sandy wastes, waiting for death to overtake them, when suddenly the cry for help of a near-by woman or child so startled the instinctive sense of duty within the heart of the traveler that he stumbled on, bearing undreamed-of burdens.

C. E. Montague has a similar story of a man upon whose defenseless head were heaped troubles beyond endurance. His wife died just as he was recovering from a gas attack in the war. His son and daughter each contracted a loveless marriage and were hopelessly disillusioned. One morning the man awoke to find that he had suffered a slight stroke. What was there in life for him? Everything was shattered. He would not kill himself, but resolved to follow a favorite but dangerous pastime of his and climb a near-by Alpine mountain. This time he would select one that had never been conquered by man. If he succeeded in reaching the top, well and good. If he failed, it was a good way to die for a man who had lost the zest for living. He almost succeeded. But near the top he found that his strength was so nearly gone that he could not cut the last few steps. He waited for a moment. Either he would die there, or he would slip and plunge into a crevasse. Suddenly he heard the cry of a woman in fear or pain above him. Miraculously his strength seemed to return to him, and he cut the last few steps and reached her as she dangled in the air, saving both her and her husband.

That sort of thing may have some complicated psychological explanation. With that we are not concerned. The simple truth, upon which we may lay hold for everyday living, is that the man who hears the calls that force themselves into his consciousness and then makes an honest effort to answer them will find an unusual strength is his portion. It is when we neglect the calls, when we convince ourselves that our share of the burden is more than we can carry, that we fail to live up to our heritage. Duty at times is a strenuous concept, for its demands are not slack; but it is a concept that bears with it a promise. In the promise we find our refuge and strength.

Let this further word be added: duty need not involve heroics or sensational deeds. Wherever a man is willing to accept the crosses of every day, he is a follower of the One who walked with slow and measured tread the path that led up the hill. Common duties have an eternal place in the scheme of the world. A proper conception of their importance will provide for us a way of escape from their crushing power. They can become windows for the soul, from which one may look across the whole landscape of life with understanding eyes.

Dr. Paul Scherer quotes the following letter in one of his sermons:

I am only fifty-five, but my body feels eighty. So much to be done, and so little strength for the doing. Thursday is my day at the specialist's, and on Friday the sky often seems very dark, and Christ far away. I am in the house alone all through the week, from six in the morning until nine at night. But whenever I read something from the New Testament I seem to get back my courage. Today I canned twelve quarts of tomatoes. That makes fifty-nine for me in all. Your work and mine are different, but I try to believe that I have a part in God's plan, and I will try to fill it as best I can. I must lie on my bed now and rest.[2]

Gallant soul that she is, she has discovered for herself that duty is the interpreter of human power.

III

There is yet another aspect of the matter. Duty is ultimately the interpreter of our relationship to God. Frequently it falls out in our human living that the affairs of the day which must be done are beyond our power to do them, no matter how wholeheartedly we give ourselves to the task, no matter how often our reserves are called up because of the extra demand of the moment. There come times in the living of each of us when we can do no more, and we must cast the burden upon one who is wiser than we. Jesus himself in following the path of duty that was laid out before him gave his spirit into the care and keeping of the Father God. He had done his part; there came a moment when duty and God became inextricably woven together in his pain-fogged thinking. Because God was woven into the tapestry, it became a thing of beauty forever, and the cross became a symbol of triumph. Duty alone could not have done it, for Jesus could not have borne the cross that way.

[2] *Facts That Undergird Life*, Harper & Bros., 1938, p. 148.

God alone could not have done it, for the meaning of the cross finds its inception in duty. Together they made man's salvation reality.

Here is a lesson that will stand many of us in good stead. Life is always confronting us with new situations, and too often we have not the ability to meet them. Duty calls us to follow a certain path, and we have not the strength or fortitude to walk all the way. Consequently, life becomes complicated, and we forfeit our birthright as human beings. God is forever flinging a challenge at us, and whether or not we are able to meet that challenge depends, in large measure, upon our inclination to lay hold of his strength. For, view life as we may, we are forced to an inevitable conclusion that God has given us an impossible task. It is our duty to be perfect creatures, and only one Being in the universe can attain that goal. If you and I were perfect, we would be equal with God. It is an impossible and, at the same time, an insistent demand.

There is a story of a keen-minded father whose little girl was a perpetual source of anxiety to him. She was a very self-important little miss, quite confident of her abilities in every field. The trait was amusing in the child but would be impossible in the woman. Wisely the father took steps to correct it. One summer, while the family was vacationing in the White Mountains, he suggested to his daughter that they climb to the top of one of the near-by hills. The child was delighted at the prospect of climbing with her father, and readily agreed. Blithely she set out on the journey. So long as the road was wide and the climbing easy, she was all eagerness. But then the road became a trail, later a tiny path. The climbing was difficult, and thorns and bushes stretched out hands to scratch and draw blood. The stones underneath made their sharp points felt through her shoes. Suddenly she tripped over a root and fell headlong. Grimly she rose, with a smudgy bruise on one side of her cheek, and tears in her eyes. But she kept on. At last after a particularly ugly fall she got up completely discouraged and chastened. Unhesitatingly she flung herself into her father's arms for protection and help. Now all was changed. She climbed with him now, instead of alone, and happily they reached the summit. The father had given his daughter an insight into one of the central truths of life. Our task is impossible alone, but in company with our Father we may stand upon heaven's tableland.

In no sense is this an exhortation to lessen anyone's conception of the duties incumbent upon him. To pray for tasks equal to one's powers is a sacrilege; to pray for powers equal to one's tasks can become a sacrament. The wise thing for many of us to do is to take stock of ourselves in these curious days in order that we may discover just what is our place in the world of men. It may not be nearly as important or outstanding as we may have hoped, but it is ours, and none other can fill it for us. Having conceived of our duty in the proper manner, let us take another step by going as far as we are able in meeting its demands. Unfortunately, here a great many lose their way! They take stock, and decide that what they have is not enough and the whole idea of service had best be abandoned. When Jesus was preparing the hearts of his audience for the miracle of feeding five thousand people with five loaves and two fishes, he asked the disciples how much food they had. One answered, glumly, "Five barley loaves and two small fishes. But what are they among so many?" It was a natural answer, but it left out of account the one fact that made the difference between success and failure—Jesus Christ. This man was ready to quit when, in reality, he had just reached the starting place. So long as men do their part, God will provide the answers to their problems, even if it takes a miracle to do it.

Much of your success in building a life structure will depend on your answer to the constant call that duties of various sorts make upon you. What the sun does depends upon the soil and the seed. The violet takes a little and responds with perfume. The oak takes a great deal and responds with timber for ships. Jesus came to show us the success that could be achieved by an entire surrender to the demands of duty. He came to offer us the sun of his righteousness and power, and to promise that where he is, there we may be also. In the strength of that promise we accept the duties of the day, being confident in our hearts that "he that spared not his own Son, but delivered him up for us all, shall with him also freely give us all things."

THE CROSS AND FAITH

And Jesus answering saith unto them, Have faith in God.—Mark 11:22.

PAUL, IN HIS MATCHLESS HYMN OF LOVE, REMINDS us that faith is one of the three imperishable attitudes of spirit which a man may assume. He who has insight into the ways of life chooses to make these three a part of his spiritual equipment, for the experience of the race is abundant proof of their necessity in the development of the best-rounded character. Illustrations might be multiplied to show that courageous and positive faith is an absolute minimum in happy existence, and hope and love find their roots oftentimes in such an attitude of belief. Jesus reminded his listeners that they who had faith would discover the treasures of heaven opening before them, while they who had no faith would find that life is dull and drab and without essential significance.

In these days of war and disturbance of every sort, when men are seeking something which will point the way to a fuller and richer life, there is no attitude of mind or heart more essential than a positive and abiding faith. That it will require the removal of some obstacles on our part is readily admitted, but the resulting faith is so rewarding that all difficulties are swept aside before the power of its entrance. It is not always easy to believe, because belief presupposes thinking, and that for some of us is a hazardous process at best. There are multiple distractions that tend to destroy our faith; and that adds to the difficulty of believing. There is always the apparent reasonableness of error that makes true faith stagger at times. Good and evil are so mixed in our scheme of things that too often we are not able to separate the two, and the good that we would believe that do we not accept because we have not the ability to draw the fine line of distinction.

None of these things escaped the Master. Above all others, he had his faith tested as by fire upon the cross. Time and again in his earthly pilgrimage he was called aside by subtle temptations to accept a short cut to power. Time and again his enemies would have ceased their plaguing of him had he been willing to compromise just a bit. But Jesus had that unconquerable, unquenchable, unmovable faith that never wavered or broke before the storms of persecution, suffering, and mistreatment of every sort. As he hung on the cross he proclaimed for us some of the undergirding principles of faith. I should like to suggest three of them for your consideration.

I

First, there is the proposition that material welfare alone does not make life meaningful. Jesus

66

had those things at his command, for did he not say that he could ask his Father for twelve legions of angels and he would send them? Did Jesus the Son of God, have to submit himself to the ignominy and disgrace which was heaped upon him by a band of brutal soldiers? Was he forced to accept the jeers and mockery of a crowd of people who were not worthy to unlatch his shoe? We all are quite assured that as we believe this Strange Man was God, so did he have the power of God, and could have accepted a much different way of ending his career upon the earth had he so chosen.

Jesus chose to suffer the cross because he believed in something. He chose it because he knew that life is not ever bounded by things that we see. He chose it because he was convinced in his own thinking that an ounce of faith is worth a pound of the more tangible things that we see and enjoy for the moment, but which perish like the flower with the passing hours. Faith in the ultimacy of a program of God, faith in the conviction that his sacrifice would not be in vain, faith in the unseen powers of righteousness and goodness—these were the things that held the Christ upon the cross. And these are the things that are being forced in upon our consciousness today with increasing urgency.

For a score of years we were building upon the belief that if a man could accumulate enough of this world's goods, and build his castle strong enough to repel the invader, then nothing more would be required. He could sit back, eat, drink, and be merry, and take his ease amid the luxury that his own ingenuity had provided. Frantically men sought for just such an existence, and it left them "fed up at fifteen and fagged out at forty." For the program did not work, and now more and more men everywhere are coming to ask the question seriously, "I wonder if faith in God is the answer after all?" Just as the magnificent Hindenburg line proved utterly worthless when manned by those who had no inner fortification, so have all Hindenburg lines of our personal experiences found themselves utterly lacking in ability to cope with modern world situations. Books such as *Life Begins at Forty*, *Wake Up and Live*, *The Return to Religion* find wide sales because people are eagerly grasping at every straw, trying to find something or somebody who can rekindle their burnt-out enthusiasm and hopes, and build back into living the "music and the dream."

We are gradually coming to know the necessity of believing in something more solid and lasting than the ephemeral things upon which we too hastily built all our hopes in the past. As Dr. Sockman points out, we thought that we were living in God's world, with quotation marks around the words, and that nothing could happen to blast our dreams of joy. Africa and Asia were pagan, but we were sending our missionaries among them and hoped to have them all converted within a generation or so. England was the seat of an empire on which the sun never set; France was the tourist's paradise; Germany was the seat of continental learning, and our more learned men went to the great universities there for graduate work, to come home more nonunderstandable than ever. America had "Coolidge prosperity," and nothing seemed amiss with the very pretty world in which we found ourselves. To be sure, there was a rumbling noise beneath it all, as injustice and oppression of many kinds made themselves audible in their effects upon the masses of the world. But we did not hear it; the material things were too dear to our hearts.

Now all that is swept away, and we realize that most of it was

> . . . . a tale
> Told by an idiot, full of sound and fury,
> Signifying nothing

But it has not been without its devastating effects. Listen to the words of one of my own generation:

The earliest memories I can recall are those of cutting out war pictures when I was a lad of eight. Then I was sent to school and college in the booming hectic twenties, graduating from Harvard in 1929, just at the peak of prosperity. Then I, with my generation of graduates, was tossed into the depression. I have never lived through what you would call normal times. What I need is something to believe in, something to hold on to.

Men must learn to see the invisible, which is beyond the material, if they are to find the happiness that seems so far away at times. Just as I might walk through beds of flowers with a gardener and have niceties of species pointed out to my unseeing eye, so may we walk through this garden of life and find that the Guide can show us many things we had not thought existed, if only we are ready to believe. Seeing the invisible is the faith we need.

II

My second proposition is closely akin to its predecessor; faith is forever necessary to the successful accomplishment of any great venture. Jesus could not have finished the work which his Father gave him to do unless he had possessed a faith beyond our ability to understand. The man who lacks faith of a similar nature does not have the inner compulsion to force him through the necessary hardships and discouragements. The one sees that which might be and therefore is willing to bend every effort to the accomplishment of that goal, no matter how distasteful or humiliating may be the steps in between; the other sees little more than the difficulty of the moment and therefore is unwilling to bear with the strain. In order for men to live nobly there must be a belief that noble living has some reward for them. Religion must show its utilitarian side or we care little for it. Faith is the binding cord between that which is and that which can be on the morrow.

This thought is true in every field of secular living. There is so little that is actually knowledge and so much that is really faith in our ordinary pursuits of living. When I was in school I studied, rather halfheartedly, a little chemistry. Today I have forgotten all but the simplest of the formulae, and have no understanding of the processes whereby elements combine for the welfare and happiness of mankind. But there are others who have used these formulae and these processes to provide for humankind better food, clothing, medicines, and every sort of civilized living. Their faith in those formulae has led them along the way to great discoveries. I also studied a little trigonometry in school. The sines and cosines, tangents and cotangents, and all the attendant formulae of mathematics, were of daily concern to me at that time. Even today I do not doubt the facts which were given me at that time. I still believe that the tables of logarithms are correct, but I have never had an occasion to make use of them. I have never written a sermon on the subject, or made them the topic of conversation on some pastoral visit. But there are those who have taken these tables and used them to throw a bridge across a chasm, to build a road through the wilderness, to make the desert blossom with roses, to send a ship arching its way across trackless wastes of water. Faith in trigonometry is to the engineer a part of the ordinary usage of everyday, and he accomplishes things by means of this faith.

That is the sort of thing to which I call you in the religious realm. If we believe in God it will not help us to build bridges (although I think it would insure the public against faulty bridge-building); it will not help us to bake our pies or manage our households or control an office force—if by help we mean that we shall be able to sit back and wait for instructions from God. Faith in God is ultimately resolvable into a firmer faith in self, because God is in us. Faith in God is a goad that prompts us to try again and again when we have failed; to accept complete defeat, because we believe that God can bring good even out of evil. Thus faith, even though it be incomplete, takes some of the mystery out of life, and changes it from "a paralyzing enigma to an adventure with the hope of justifying outcome." Coventry Patmore is reported when only eleven years of age to have been struck while reading with a sudden thought, "What an exceedingly fine thing it would be if there really was a God." It is an exceedingly fine thing to believe there is a God, for out of that belief come the accomplishments that make this world of ours livable.

Any account of the make-up of a human being

has no right to leave out of consideration those things that are the so-called imponderables of life. We cannot say that a man is so much sugar, so much phosphorus, so much iron, and such. That sort of an equation may express satisfactorily the chemical qualities of a man, but it does not allow for that which is fundamentally the possession of man only —his spiritual abilities. There are factors in the life of a man that we do not measure, no matter how completely we know his weight and height and color and physical characteristics. The *New York Times* expressed the emptiness of the victory of Hitler over the city of Paris in the following words:

It is only the lovely shell that Hitler has captured. He has not captured the true Paris. Never can he, his tanks, his robot battalions penetrate within the walls of that magic city. Paris where democracy had its modern rebirth; Paris that taught the world to paint and build; Paris of museums, libraries, universities in which the mind could range at will; Paris the spiritual, Paris the city of love, Paris the city of light . . . . this is not Hitler's Paris, not today or ever.

The Louvre, the Sorbonne, Notre Dame—they are more than buildings. They are backed by imponderable elements of life that make them meaningful. In human life it is not different. There must be the quality of faith infusing and diffusing itself through every avenue of existence if there are to come the great victories that we long to see.

III

So we have arrived naturally at the climax of the matter: faith is something that must enter the human heart of the volition of that heart. We cannot line up people and inoculate them with a "shot" of faith; we cannot pour a spoonful and suggest that every ailing and aching heart take this medicine. Faith as a quality of the spirit must become a personal possession, and that takes place only through conviction that the object of faith is real and abiding. The old definitions that faith is believing the impossible have found their way to the wastebasket. In faith we are called upon to believe that which we cannot understand, but we know that God is, and that is sufficient for a practical faith content.

This sort of thing cannot be shared by two persons. I might outline for you that which I believe, and you might tell me things in which you have put your faith, but finally we would discover that there are some things each accepts which are denied by the other. Faith is not a matter of being told what to believe—we cannot do it that way even if we would. We may learn of others that which people have believed, and we may inquire diligently into the reasons for this, and then at last we may be convinced that it is worth believing; but that last step is ours alone. This is one thing that gives reality to the faith of men, and makes it the goading, guiding dynamic of living.

Jesus points us to the truth of this in the last few hours upon the cross. Seven times he spoke from the cross, and the two deepest expressions of his agony were intensely personal: "Why hast thou forsaken me?" and "Father, into thy hands I commend my spirit." The first of these was the admission that his faith was tested to the breaking point. The latter is the triumphant assertion that his faith had been strong enough to meet the test and was confident of the future. But each of them was from the heart of one man alone at a crisis in his living. Each of these is an expression, in its way, of that which was taking place within his spirit, never that of another.

So it becomes dangerous to suggest too minutely the content of faith that will suffice for you. Some, such as Gerald Heard, accept the idea of a "Plastic Universe," and believe that man can live up to any standards of goodness he sets for himself; others believe but vaguely in man's goodness and long for some merging into cosmic consciousness. Still others accept at its face value that which the Bible says—"Ask, and it shall be given you; seek, and ye shall find; knock, and it shall be opened unto you"— and to them it is just as simple as that; we need nothing more than a complete faith in God as Father and the whole of the jigsaw puzzle will fit itself into place.

Faith must become a personal possession and must be wrought out on the anvil of one's own thinking. The sparks that fly therefrom may serve to kindle the enthusiasm of others, but the complete product belongs only to its maker. Faith of that sort is worth while, for it has cost the man who has it. Only those things that do cost are worth anything to the world.

Yes, there are things in our world that will not die, and all the hell of shot and shell will not erase them. For the moment the clouds are more powerful than the sun, but we know the sun is still there, and in that confidence we step out into every tomorrow that shall be granted us. Faith has made life what it is for good; faith shall build more stately mansions for the future, if we are strong enough to follow its leading.

James Hilton has written a number of interesting works. Not least among them are two that contrast in central idea. *Lost Horizon*, you remember, is a story of a mythical Shangri-La where all the lovely and beautiful things of human living are preserved. It was a beautiful dream, and it had its appeal to many of us. But in another book Mr. Hilton created a character whom he called Mr. Chips, whose beauty of soul and breadth of living made itself felt through the troublous days of the World War. And you and I know that Shangri-La will never be until we have enough Mr. Chipses to make it so. That is our task as Christians. The happiness of unborn generations depends upon our response. What is yours?

76

THE CROSS AND HOPE

For we are saved by hope.—Rom. 8:24.

DR. FOSDICK DRAWS ATTENTION TO AN OLD VOLUME of theology in which the table of contents starts in this manner, "Chapter One, Hell; Chapter Two, Hell Continued." We know the deepest meaning of that statement. Two world wars within one lifetime certainly might be classified as "Hell" and "Hell Continued." The strain attendant upon such catastrophic happenings is not without its telling effect upon each of us. Not only are we deprived of many of the luxuries of living because of the necessity of war effort, but also there is enforced upon us a nervous tension that threatens to wear down the edge of happy living. Some of us are afraid; some of us are anxious for loved ones; some of us are concerned for future prosperity; some of us are almost hopeless.

To such conditions the Christian church makes bold to speak. During these Lenten days our thoughts are particularly turned back across the centuries to stirring days of long ago, when, amid the blackness of the human depravity of another generation, a Man who held the hope of the world within his hands was led forth to die. With striking reality it is borne in upon us that the Jesus in

77

whom the disciples trusted so implicitly was nailed to the rough and splintery arms of a cross of a to-talitarian despot. Suffering as we do from similar exhibitions of the apparent triumph of the forces of evil, we do well to turn our thoughts to this event which shook the world.

Ibsen has a drama which he entitles *The Emperor and the Galilean*. In this play Julian the Apostate is represented as having a dream in which he fancied himself carried to another planet, from which he looked down upon the earth where he had destroyed Christianity and rooted out the name of Jesus Christ. Listen!

But behold, there came a procession by me on the strange earth, where I stood. There were soldiers and judges and executioners at the head of it, and weeping women followed. And lo, in the midst of the slow-moving array was the Galilean—alive, and bearing a cross on His back. Then I called to Him and I said, "Whither away, Galilean?" and He turned His face to me and smiled and nodded slowly and said, "To the place of the skull."

We never escape from Jesus. He cannot be disposed of as easily as some of his enemies have imagined. The cross is still the focal point for the redemption of mankind—it is still the center of the hope that is left for us. This Christ of the cross returns again and again to haunt our thinking and to fill to the brim the cup of hope from which we all wish to drink satisfying draughts in such days.

Apart from him we find little in which to hope, for life becomes constricted and narrow and bound about with the pettiness of our desires and ambitions. We are lost amid the manifold detail of living and become hopeless of finding a way out of the maze. But, reminded of the cross, we are able to take heart once more, and hope becomes vibrant within our breasts.

I

This is true because the experience of Jesus on the cross shows us the necessity of viewing the events of life against a larger background than is afforded by ordinary experience. Had Jesus looked upon the terrifying experience of the cross as merely one event in which he was to be the principal actor, it may well have been that he would have refused to go through with it. The disciples failed to establish this larger background; consequently they were almost destroyed by the tragic events of Black Friday. Certainly they were demoralized, and it required over a month for them to regain their lost confidence in Jesus.

Human experience is understandable only when we see it as a whole. We cannot select this or that part of it and be perturbed beyond measure because of it. Whatever happens to humankind must be seen with its large background, with the experiences of a lifetime woven into the fabric of the moment. To be sure, there are moments when it will

seem almost impossible that we do this sort of thing.
Life has its own way of sending a flood tide of sorrow and disaster hurtling down upon our defenseless heads. But there is no other method of meeting such moments with confidence and hope.

Bishop Fiske has a story which illustrates the point. One summer many years ago he and a group of friends were fishing in Maine. One of the men was an astronomer and another was a geologist. The guide who accompanied them was a rock-ribbed Maine Republican, and that summer he was particularly concerned lest William Jennings Bryan win his race for the presidency. What would happen to the country if a Democrat should get to the White House? More particularly, what would happen to the nation if a Democrat such as Bryan were elected? One night the five men were seated around a campfire, and the astronomer and the geologist were discussing the age of the universe. The astronomer gave some unusual illustrations of the distances that were involved in this universe of ours. Then the geologist talked at length about the rocks and the ages of time that were necessary for the formation of the various strata that we know. The guide was dumfounded by the facts to which he was listening. Never before had he known that any such things as these were true. He was not wholly convinced of them even yet, but he had heard enough to crystallize one thought in his mind. He put it into words as he said, "Well, I guess it won't make a powerful lot of difference if William Jennings Bryan is elected president." Against the background of eternity, as these men had pictured it, one president more or less made little difference.

We need an outlook of this sort today. We are so concerned about our present difficulties that we have failed to take into account the background from which they are taken. The affairs of the moment seem so immensely important that we have not the time or the inclination to view them as merely part of a scheme. The importance of the minute of time through which we are passing seems to outweigh all the hours that have preceded.

Not that we should ever attempt to deny the importance of the present. After all, we do live at the moment. Our pains and travail are not less severe because we remind ourselves that the world is an old, old place. But somehow they are more bearable when we indulge this larger viewpoint. There does appear a meaning hidden away at the heart of all things, and in that meaning we rest our hopes, knowing that it is of God. Our problems of national and international life are more solvable when we see that we are not the first generation to face a situation such as this. Our domestic problems assume much less of an impossible outlook when we place them over against the history of the nation. All of the difficulties that stare us in the face have been met with stolid fortitude by men and women before us. Oftentimes with much less ability, with fewer gifts, with far less opportunity, they were able to win through to glorious victories. Can we do less? Against the background of a larger span of time the affairs of the day fall into place more readily, and we are confident that "all things work together for good." Get a long-range perspective and life will seem much more meaningful —hope will blossom much more significantly.

II

Yet again we find that the cross is a symbol of hope for humankind because it forever reminds us that the impossible becomes the possible with God. As men looked upon the limp Figure hanging wearily, agonizingly, upon that cross they thought that it was impossible for any influence to radiate from such a defeated man. His followers would not dare, or care, to remember his name. Grievously had he disappointed them; hopelessly had he allowed the soldiers to nail him to the tree; the future was impossible of producing any good as far as he was concerned. He was dead—there is nothing more impossible than life out of death!

But his tormentors reckoned without God. He who does so is ignorant of the deeper currents of human living. We all have to do with this Being who first sent the planets spinning into space and who breathed into us the breath that made us living souls. We cannot escape him, though we flee him

down the halls of time, and take cover in the soli-
tude of space. He is always there, and we do not
rid ourselves of him. Those who recognize this
fact for the possibilities inherent within it lay hold
upon that which becomes a solid rock on which to
build every worth-while hope for the morrow.

No matter how impossible the future may seem
to you, remember that God's arm is not yet shorten-
ed, and that he has always done the impossible when
it has been for the good of his children. We have
the right to expect great things from our God. Too
often we have been timid in our hopes for the future. Let us look out with eyes and hearts open to
the things that might take place, instead of holding
to the constricting, devastating, destructive idea
that the world has now come to an end and there is
nothing that can be done about it. Man's extrem-
ity is forever God's opportunity, and we rejoice in
the exigencies of the moment, for "when we are
weak, then are we strong" through this power of
the eternal God.

However, let a word of caution be injected here.
Let us not come to think of God as merely a servant
of ours who is waiting to do our bidding. That
conception of the power and value of prayer is de-
grading to God and shaming to us. He is not our
genie to be summoned by the rubbing of the magic
lamp of prayer. Those things for which we ask
may be withheld from us, according to his knowledge of our good or ill. Someone said recently that

during the World War President Wilson appointed a day of prayer, and that the German armies were not able to make a single advance after that. The retreat that ended in disaster began shortly after the American people had called upon God for victory.

But that sort of thing raises questions at times. Why did not a similar happening take place when the German armies marched into Poland in the fall of 1939? A good cause was at stake, as we are able to see it, and a few days of rain would have proved to be the effective resistance that the Polish battalions were not. Did God not hear the prayers that were offered at this time, or was he impotent to do anything about it?

Let me suggest that we keep this thought in mind. God is able, but he may not do what we ask. The "impossibility" of the moment may not be for him the time that he should loose "the fateful lightning of his terrible swift sword," and therefore he keeps it sheathed. But someday there will come a moment when the heavens shall part, and those things that we had thought could not be shall be brought to pass by a power beyond our ken. I am frank to confess that I find God working mightily in the world in such events as the golden era of Augustus in Rome, the victory of the barons at Runnymede, the overthrow of the French monarchy or Coolidge prosperity. I am also frank to confess that I believe such things as these stem not from themselves, not from the moment, but from the long-range view of history that our God maintains. "He also serves who only stands and waits" is not without its application to the Father God. He who has faith can be well assured of the morrow, for he knows that God can change the impossible of today into the fact of tomorrow—if it is his will.

III

So we have come to the crux of the entire matter. For him who has faith to see beyond the cross into the Easter dawn there is always hope, no matter how impossible may seem the moment. When Hector of Troy heard the call to battle, he went to bid farewell to Andromache and his infant son. He was ready for the fray, armed and helmeted. As he drew near the baby the child cried out and shrank away, frightened by the waving plume. Hector smiled and, laying aside the helmet, took his son and kissed him fondly. Instantly the child's fears were allayed. This was no warrior—this was his father.

Ultimately this must be our conception of God. Certainly he is a warrior, in the sense that he makes war upon evil, but he is forever the Father of wayward and erring children. We can expect good and not evil from his hand. We are not called upon to face the grim and inexorable tasks of life alone— there is One who stands by our side to lend us the sympathetic power of his presence. We are in alliance with the force of the universe when we make ready for the coming of the power of God.

Let us not go further without admitting frankly the difficulty of such faith. To believe that God is and that he is the rewarder of those who diligently seek him requires no little courage. But the world has based its slow trek upward through the mud and slime into the intelligence of humanity upon courage. It was a sure sign of courage on the part of the disciples who first agreed to entrust their all to the countryman whose name was Jesus of Nazareth. Dean Swift once said that the man who ate the first oyster took a tremendous risk of faith. That sort of thing is true with the majority of our living. There are leaps in the dark that must be taken, not because we enjoy them or find consolation in the action of leaping, but because God has told us that such is the way that the future will become meaningful to us.

Jesus knew what it was to have faith strained to the breaking point. From the depths of an agonized soul was wrung that cry from the cross, "My God, why hast thou forsaken me?" Alone at the turning point of the ages, Jesus felt that even God had failed to enter into a full fellowship of his suffering. But this was not the last word of a man who had drained to the dregs the cup of bitter human experience. Listen to him in his further word, "Father, into thy hands I commend my spirit." In that latter sentence we have the inexpressible longing of a human heart for security put into tangible form. Into the hands of God we commend that which we have and are, being quite well assured that these hopes of ours shall not be disappointed.

When we come to see the experience of Calvary in such a light we understand more clearly the idea that faith is not some abstract way of thinking, but a definite, concrete way of living—of accepting "the slings and arrows of outrageous fortune" as well as the blessings of the journey. Faith is a way of measuring up to the responsibilities of the moment with magnificent courage, with incalculable resource.

You remember, in *Through the Looking Glass*, the White Queen declared that she was one hundred and one years, five months and a day old. "I can't believe that!" said Alice. "Can't you?" the Queen said in a pitying tone. "Try again: draw a long breath, and shut your eyes." And many people view the Christian faith in such a light. Here is something that is impossible to believe. But it has helped people, apparently; therefore we will take a long breath and try again to believe something that all common sense tells us is not so. Thus confusing faith with credulity we lower it to the level of superstition. Sometimes confusing faith with magic we lower it to the realm of sorcery. Faith is a method of dealing with that which is *im*possible in a *possible* way.

Sometimes the possible way is the long one. It

could have happened that God sent the twelve legions of angels of which Jesus spoke and destroyed the Roman Empire on the day that its minions dared to nail the Son of God to a cross. There could have been lightnings from heaven that split asunder not only the veil of the temple but the entire Jewish nation. God with power could have declared that day that he was yet the sovereign ruler of the universe. Yet note how he chose to deal with the impossible situation of the crucifixion. Jesus died—a useless waste of human life from our viewpoint. Jesus rose again to appear only to his own people, not to the mobs or the Roman authorities or the Jewish leaders. For four centuries Christians were hounded and persecuted and forced to live in dens and caves of the earth. But faith was working in the hearts of the people who knew this Nazarene, and God was working in his own way to proclaim that Jesus Christ is the Ruler of all men everywhere. Not yet has the consummation of this power which had been given him made itself manifest, but we have seen enough to be quite well assured that there is no doubt that God ordereth these things as it seemeth good unto him. As an old reformer once said, "The only difference between the difficult and the impossible is that the impossible takes a little longer time."

A tremendous venture, you say, to try and believe that? Surely—an impossible venture! But then there are no impossibilities to him who places his hand in the hand of God and steps forth to meet life. An old Alpine guide saw a man trembling on the brink of a crevasse, stretched out his hand to him, and said in a strong, clear voice, "Here, man, take this hand. It has never lost a man." God speaks so to us in the midst of our wars and rumors of wars, our surging spirits, our ebbing hearts, our hopeless moments, as well as our joyful days. Have you no hope? Are you afraid? Do worries and anxieties destroy your usefulness? Listen:

I will hew great windows for my soul,
Channels of splendor, portals of release;
Out of earth's prison walls will I hew them,
That my thundering soul may push through them;
Through strata of human strife and passion
I will tunnel a way, I will carve and fashion
With the might of my soul's intensity
Windows fronting immensity,
Towering out of Time.
I will breathe the air of another clime
That my spirit's pain may cease.
That the *being* of me have room to grow,
That my eyes may meet God's eyes and know,
I will hew great windows, wonderful windows,
   measureless windows, for my soul.[1]

[1] From "Room!" in Angela Morgan, *Selected Poems*. Reprinted by permission of Dodd, Mead & Co., Inc.

THE CROSS AND LOVE

*Behold, what manner of love the Father hath
bestowed upon us.*—I John 3:1.

THE DEEPEST THINGS IN HUMAN EXPERIENCE ARE
oftentimes expressed by the simplest words. God,
life, hope, faith, love are all monosyllables, yet what
vastness they encompass in their meaning. Framed
by baby lips, their deepest significance escapes the
wisest thinker. Dealt with daily, their import is
beyond our comprehension. They are the most
familiar things of our living and the most mysteri-
ous. We do not pretend to be able to penetrate the
depths of their profound compass, and yet we are
well assured in our hearts that life would be intolerable without them.

For a season let us turn our thoughts to the deepest manifestation of one of these concepts that the
world knows. Love and the cross are linked together in a manner that baffles one who would attempt some cold analysis of the factors that made
up the drama of Calvary. We cannot say that love
is here or there, and from that point forward duty
is a controlling element. We dare not say that love
begins at this point and ends at another, for then
we have presumed to dissect the character of God
himself. The apostle states for us one of the more

90

profound thoughts of New Testament wisdom when he says, "God is love." There is no beginning or ending to these interchangeable conceptions—they are one and the same idea, and he who would understand the one must accept the other.

> We may not know, we cannot tell,
>   What pains He had to bear;
> But we believe it was for us
>   He hung and suffered there.

I

The first thing that is apparent to each one who thinks concerning this subject is that love is constant. It does not fluctuate between poles of ardent affection one day and cold rejection the next. The object of affection may be unworthy, may be "despised and rejected of men," but love keeps the flame of devotion burning upon its altar. The tragic consummation on Calvary's slope proclaims this fact in clarion tones. Had not love exercised such a moving power in the life of Jesus he could not have accomplished the work of redemption. Those whom he loved most dearly forsook him and fled away into the darkness of the night. Round him were only a few of the faithful souls who still trusted that he was the One who should redeem Israel. His disciples, his friends, his followers among the multitudes, were gone away as he hung poised between earth and sky. But he loved them enough to remain there—for their sake.

In religion, as in all of life, we are constantly concerned with those things that abide. Change and decay all about us remind us of the transitory existence that each of us has on this speck of dust called earth. We are frightened at moments by the fact that "here today and gone tomorrow" is so tragically true of our whole business of living. In spite of anything said to the contrary, we are much in love with life, and we are anxious to prolong it as long as possible. Failing in that, we certainly wish to know that there are some things which death cannot destroy, upon which we may lay hold. We are desirous that our names be remembered by those we leave behind. We are hopeful that we will be well spoken of in years to come, and pride prompts the thought that in the future our names will be ones with which to conjure.

Now a great deal of the realization of such desires will be conditioned by that which we ourselves are while we are here upon the earth. If we wish to be remembered kindly, then we must see to it that we lay the foundations for a kindly remembrance. If we wish merely to be remembered, then we must be careful that we manifest only such negative virtues as will leave behind us nothing positive, either good or bad. For men will think of us, now, as well as later, by that which they know about us—they have no other criterion.

Therefore, it is the part of wisdom to look back across the centuries and catch a vision of that incarnate Love accepting rusty spikes into quivering flesh because deep in his heart there was a constant, overpowering flame that knew no boundaries, that was inclosed by no inhibitions. Our love is so often like the ebb and flow of the tide—exuberance for the moment, a heap of dry sand a few hours later. Like summer's flowers it is born only to die, and the world is drearier because of the passing. Jesus, the ideal lover, shows us that it is possible to carry within our hearts at all times the flame that kindles sacrifice and promotes happiness. We need not fluctuate with the wind if we take him as our example in this matter.

This ideal is not as easy to attain as might appear at first. So often the objects of affection spurn our proffered gifts, and we find the rejection rankles in our heart. Our self-respect demands that we go our appointed way and refuse to have further ado with those whom we had thought to love but who will not accept that which we have to give them. Such moments are the testing period of the constancy of our devotion. To be able to continue to give when no return is expected is the hallmark of abiding love. To be able to give affection when every advance is spurned and despised is the goal of every true follower of the Christ.

Our task in the world is to spread the leaven of a new type of human relationship. Although Jesus proclaimed it two thousand years ago, it is still new because it is so utterly foreign to the human con-

93

ception of things. We are called upon to learn the secret of loving those who despise us, of praying for those who despitefully use us, of blessing those who curse us. The eye-for-an-eye type of philosophy must disappear from our world if we are to find the happiness we crave. For centuries we have tried loving those who love us, and changing with the wind of shifting affections on their part; now the time has come in the history of the race when we must seriously attempt to love men as the Master did. We must see our task of the morrow as one which demands the deepest consecration of which we are capable, for it is no easy undertaking to love those who have mistreated us. But it can be done, and the world waits with bated breath for a solution of its problems. The old methods have all failed. International law, education, commerce, planned economics all have proved insufficient to stem the tide of hatreds between nations—why not begin a Christian program that promises to love all men regardless of what takes place? It would be a radical departure from the old idea of "if you love me I will love you," but it might prove to be the very panacea for which humanity is so desperately seeking. Certainly it would be following in the steps of the gentle Jesus.

II

In the second place we are reminded by the cross that love is forever the most selfless thing with

THE CROSS AND LOVE

which we have to do. Hope invariably is twined about with some desire for self; faith is a combination of factors that have to do with one's own personality; but love is the virtue that forgets self in the larger desire that wells up within the heart for the person loved. In that thought is one of the reasons why he who loves approaches more nearly to the character of God than any other. For the man who has loved knows the utter rejection of selfish desires. Love demands of him who feels its moving currents within that nothing else be quite so important as the object of affection.

Before Jesus went out to Gethsemane and its agonies he and the disciples had a heart-to-heart conversation. It is one of the most revealing incidents that we have of the heart of the Master. One of the things that he said to those who were so dear to him was this: "If ye loved me, ye would rejoice." He was to return to his Father's house of many mansions—those who truly loved him would be overwhelmingly happy that this was true. Their thoughts at the moment were of their own personal loss, and Jesus reminded them that this cannot ever serve as a true criterion of love. For them the immediate future was uncertain, but the Man of Sorrows was showing them a picture of the gates of heaven opening for him. A stronger love for him would have dried their tears and filled them with joy as they waited for the consummation of his promise that he would return unto them.

How glibly we say this and how far we are from proving its truth! But he who fails to set idealisms, even in love, does not reach for the highest. Possession is but a part of love, and he who has learned the deepest secret of its mighty power no longer thinks of some object of affection as being possessed by him, but as being merely loved by him. There is a letter which Dorothy Whitney Straight wrote to Herbert Croly shortly after the death of her husband, Willard Straight, which sets this forth in words beyond compare.

But just because he taught me to see life with new eyes, just because he liberated my spirit and brought me life and the abundance of it, now that he is gone I cannot feel that the meaning and joy of existence have gone, too. Had he given me less I should find myself less equipped to meet life without him now. But having given me everything, I can still feel that life is the adventure that he revealed, the quest for reality that he enjoyed, the great enterprise in which he so vigorously and gallantly participated.[1]

In the above letter we find a key that may serve to unlock many of the doors that we have thought effectively shut to us. We have too long considered love as being, in its essence, acquisition and possession, and little enough of selflessness. Consequently we have set barriers about it, and have shut ourselves and others within those barriers, not always

[1] H. D. Croly, *Willard Straight*, The Macmillan Co., 1924, p. 568.

THE CROSS AND LOVE

realizing that by so doing we are destroying the
very thing that we wish to keep. It is no new insight that prompts these observations—it is as old
as human life, but each generation must discover
for itself the deep truth that is inherent in the center of love's possibilities. It is the one thing in the
world that we must give away in order to keep,
must renounce in order to hold. Some have been
able to attain such a standard, and they have found
a joy within their spirits that they had not dreamed
of hitherto. Love in its purity is so utterly selfless that the greatest fears of life are destroyed before its power.

Dr. Clovis G. Chappell, in one of his inimitable
sermons, tells of a lad who went as a recruit to a
Civil War regiment. He was unattractive and un-
couth in every possible way. He could not handle
a musket; he could scarcely walk a straight line
without falling over his own feet. He was naturally the butt of many jokes and jibes on the part of
his companions, for the perversity of human nature seems to express itself more often against weaker members of the tribe than any other. But one
officer befriended the boy. He saw that the mis-
takes the lad made were beyond his control, and he
did what he could to make up to him for that which
the others were doing. But if the boy appreciated
it he never let it be known, and not a word of
thanks fell from his lips.

One night the regiment was sleeping without

tents in the bitter cold of midwinter. The officer shivered under his one blanket, trying to sleep. Finally a delightful sense of warmth stole over him and he drifted off to sleep. When he awakened a few hours later he discovered that he had two blankets spread over him. At first he was without an explanation, but then he noticed some distance away the green, gawky, unattractive soldier whom he had befriended, walking about swinging his thin arms across his body, trying to keep from freezing to death. The boy died a few days later of exposure which he suffered that night. But, as he died, there was a smile on his lips, for beside him sat the officer whom, in his own way, that boy deeply loved.[2] Love just does not count the cost, for self is always last.

III

There is one further thought in regard to this mighty power of love with which we have to do. Oftentimes it assumes unrecognizable forms, and we are left wondering, for the moment, if the love that we had expected to find is really there at all. The night that Jesus gathered with his disciples in the upper room was one of the most difficult experiences through which humans have passed. A yearning, brooding heart of love reached out to those men who were round about him, and a de-

[2] *Sermons on Biblical Characters*, George H. Doran Co., 1922, p. 50.

termination to fulfill the highest reaches of that love forced him to announce his decision of a separation from them. They simply could not grasp the significance of his decision and through the long hours of his trial and death they were still nonplused that he should have deserted them as he did. It did not occur to them that they had deserted him by failing to believe that love such as he had shown them was seeking only the deepest interests of their lives.

The disciples could not understand why it was that One who professed to love them should leave them. That very misunderstanding twisted as one of the knives that pierced the breast of the Master. Gethsemane would have been easier, Calvary would have been more bearable, if those whom Jesus loved more dearly than any other—if one is able to compare divine love—had accepted that which he was doing as the highest manifestation of his affection for them. Caesar, wrapped in a blood-stained mantle, died at the base of Pompey's statue, of a broken heart. The cruelty of his friends had killed him, not their swords. The nature of Jesus was forced to undergo a more profound grief as he watched those whom he had nurtured and lived with for three years totally misunderstand him.

"Nevertheless . . . . it is expedient for you that I go away. . . . . Arise, let us go hence." So into the garden, where the Passover moon was sending its first experimental rays, went a little company of men. Amid the darkness of the shadows of the olive trees, Jesus poured out his soul in its measureless love and devotion. The waves of suffering flowed along all the paths of the garden. A Man was wrestling with hosts of adversaries seeking to turn him from his appointed path. Through the fields of the sky they came, their armor reflecting the light of the stars and the pale Syrian moon. But Jesus bared his breast to receive the blow. He knew that love must sometimes do that which is unrecognizable. He wanted to stay with these men who had been so close to him, but the same desire that prompted that thought drove him on to leave them through Calvary's gate.

In such a thought there is much comfort for us. In our human relations we have had the lesson driven home to us time and again. From infancy we have had moments when we could not understand the course of events that professed love for us was assuming. We can well remember being deprived of certain pleasures that at the time were deemed indispensable, and at the moment we were quite concerned as to the reality of affection that could be so cruel and heartless. Along the trails of memory there loom also occasional vivid reminders of parental belief in the old adage "To spare the rod is to spoil the child." At the time it was a rather serious matter to a youthful mind that love could assume such utterly unrecognizable forms. The years have convinced one who has

100

since known the joys of parenthood that such times in his experience were in many respects the deepest evidence of love that could have been adduced.

So often, with a total misunderstanding of the nature of God, we have placed the blame for every catastrophe that strikes us squarely upon his shoulders, as though he derived some sadistic pleasure from inflicting pain upon helpless creatures. Even though we ourselves are often to blame for the things that happen, we continually ask in derision, "Why does God allow these things to happen if he loves us?" The answer is simple enough when we probe for it. These things happen *because* God loves us, and that love assumes forms which we in our earthly blindness are not able to recognize as the deepest affection possible. Every human sorrow is a sorrow to God; every blow that we suffer wounds him to the quick; every heartache that engulfs us strikes also to the heart of the gentle, loving, patient God.

We cannot reduce life to its simplest forms without including in its make-up the force of love. We cannot discuss the relationships between God and man without making the essence of that discussion love. Its power, its reality, its abilities, are not gainsaid, or discarded by contemptuous sallies. We do not measure the aspects of love—it simply comes flowing into our lives like a great tide that sweeps all before the might of its reality. We do not enclose it with mathematical figures, nor encompass it with chemical formulae. We merely know it, feel it, and our lives are stronger because of its certainty. As this thought lays hold upon us, the transcendent splendor of God himself is revealed, for "God is love," and those who have discovered the fact for themselves need no further answer to life. The only reaction is one of immediate and honest simplicity in responding to the heartbeat of the Infinite.

Tennyson lived in the western country, where there was a river whose waters rose with the tides of the sea. Inrushing waters flooded muddy banks miles inland, and the grounded helpless boats proudly floated upon the bosom of the tide. On every hand, that calm tide made itself felt in the sweep of its grandeur, the power of its movement. The poet saw it with understanding eyes:

But such a tide as moving seems asleep,
Too full for sound and foam,
When that which drew from out the boundless deep
Turns again home.

So love flows! Flooding the barren inlets, redeeming the muddy flats, floating the vessels of hope and joy, love is a power that will yet transform the earth.

THE CROSS AND SUFFERING

*For I reckon that the sufferings of this present
time are not worthy to be compared with the
glory which shall be revealed in us.*—Rom. 8:18.

AN ADEQUATE PHILOSOPHY OF LIFE MUST TAKE INTO
account the fact of suffering. To ignore that
which occupies such a prominent place in the life
of each of us is to admit one's inability to face the
facts of human existence as they are. The philosophies that have attempted to deny the reality of
suffering have had their day; sooner or later disillusionment creeps into the soul of the man or woman who follows such shallow teachings. As much as
we might like to deny the reality of many things
that are present in the world, we do little more
than break ourselves upon the rocks of truth when
we make the effort. Suffering is here, and we do
much better to face the fact than to try to find some
hiding place from it.

Having made such an admission, an inevitable
question follows—"Why?" If the universe is the
friendly place that so many of its students have con-
tended that it is, why should the burdens of every
day be heaped upon us? More particularly, why
should it happen that some men are singled out for
peculiar torture, and their bodies or spirits twisted

mercilessly upon racks of agony? Read the paper any day and you find a cross section of misery that threatens to negate all that love can do. And there simply is no glib and easy answer to it all. For centuries men have cast about in their thinking, seeking to devise some reasonable explanation for it all; and none has yet emerged. The problem is too big for our words to encompass it, or for our minds to comprehend it.

However, this does not mean that there is no answer. Christianity would have no eternal appeal did it neglect to state some considerations in regard to this, the greatest problem of human experience. If our finite minds are not able fully to comprehend the answers, then we can do nothing wiser than cast the entire problem in the lap of God and trust firmly that there is an answer somewhere. To those who insist that this is begging the question, I can only point out that the deepest things in human living must be accepted on faith, for there is no explanation that we can understand. Faith, hope, and love are not explainable—they are simply true. That God knows and understands the deepest significance of human suffering is the wisest way of answering many of the plaguing difficulties of life. God suffered on Calvary; God suffered in the devastating blackness of the garden. His is no hearsay experience with this phenomenon. He knows its reality; he knows its meanings. A Christian can

104

be forever confident that "all things work together for good to them that love God."

I

As we look again at the three crosses outlined bleakly against a blackened sky, we are reminded by the one which held the Master that suffering is the great common denominator of human experience. Even the Son of God was racked with pain of body and deep distress of soul. Even the Saviour of the world walked slowly through the Valley of the Shadow. It is an experience that comes to all of us soon or late. It assumes a hundred different forms, grotesque and horrible. It sits grinning at us from some vantage point that we cannot reach, and laughs at our writhings. Pain—who has not known its repulsive touch? Fear—who has not felt its clammy hand? Bereavement, sorrow, disillusionment—who has not been stricken by them? Men suffer; we cannot escape.

From an experience as universal as suffering there are many lessons that the centuries would speak to the hours. As we look about us to find some glimpses of light in a darkness so thick as to be almost tangible, we are aghast at the sheer, stark tragedy of the world. To many of us it has come home in a personal way; to all of us there are intimations that life is not good. The blackness of a world Calvary has settled about our defenseless heads, and we cry aloud before the spasms of animal fury that engulf us. What did Jesus do in his moment of deepest travail?

Well, one thing he did not do was despair and cry that all was lost because this thing had happened to him. The sufferings of Jesus will never be equaled by any human being, because the sensitive nature of his soul was such that his wounds would be far more poignant than those of the average human being. But never do we find Jesus counseling that men despair of the goodness of life. Never do we find this Man of Sorrows moaning that all is lost because he was carried down into the depths of suffering. His heart was broken; his body was lacerated; his spirit was cruelly disappointed; but still he clung to his faith in a Father God who could make all right, no matter how wrong it might be at the moment.

Our present generation finds it exceedingly difficult to maintain that outlook upon life and its more significant problems. A wave of cynicism has swept over us that has left us parched upon arid deserts of unbelief. The world has not been kind to us in many ways, and the scars of our encounters are ever with us to remind us that it has not been dreaming on our part. Again and again we have been cast into the pit, and we are wearied with the effort of climbing out. No doubt you remember the vivid passage in *All Quiet on the Western Front* where the young German soldier soliloquizes: "To-day we would pass through the scenes of our youth like travellers. We are burnt up by hard facts. . . . . We are forlorn like children, and experienced like old men, we are crude and sorrowful and superficial—I believe we are lost."

On every hand we find prophets of the future who assure us that all is lost, and that we are inevitably headed for another "gin and jazz era" in which our old people will be bewildered and our youngsters disillusioned before life's dreams have crystallized in their thinking. Demagogues will arise to lead us out of the wilderness, and they will not be without their followers among a people who have lost their hope amid the sufferings of this present age. It is a sorrowful picture, but it is not a Christian picture. If those things occur we shall suffer horribly, but if they occur they will do so in spite of the church and the soldiers of Christ. We have no part in mere acquiescence to some supposedly inevitable future. We do not despair in the midst of our suffering, because we know that "if God be for us, who can be against us?" We shall not accept the world; we shall build the world. We shall not play the game according to the rules; we shall make better rules.

If there is any attitude that is destructive to personality it is a whining acceptance of life as though we had been mistreated by some capricious deity who took delight in losing thunderbolts of misery upon our defenseless heads. After all, a comfortable world in which to exist would not offer us any challenge to meet its adversities. These experiences of pain and suffering through which we pass have a purifying effect that builds up something inside a man that links his spirit with the divine. Victory would not be sweet without the possibility of defeat; joy would not be intriguing without the possibility of pain; happiness would not be worth while without the possibility of sorrow. While we may not quite reach as high as we should like, the idea is sound that when God takes away a sun he always gives a star. Compensation is one of the established principles of life. Sometimes we are a bit puzzled just where to find that for which we are seeking, for there are moments when it seems that everything has been snatched from us by some cruel hand of Fate; but always for him who has eyes to see there are eternal values guaranteed for every moment of suffering through which we pass.

We become so interested in individual phases of living that we fail to catch the glimpse that is afforded those who wish to see it, of the common bond by which we are all bound up in this bundle of life. Oftentimes that sort of understanding is the very thing we need to make us able to withstand the darts of the enemy that are thrust at us. We may scorn the idea of sympathy being an alleviating factor in our pain and woe, but those who have been down in the Valley of agony can remember with gratitude the helping hand that was stretched out to them. It may be the child of a deep-rooted selfishness, but the fact is that it helps us to bear with these afflictions of the moment if we are aware that we are not the first persons who have been tried in such furnaces.

I once knew a lady whose husband died of typhoid fever. She told me shortly afterward that she had renounced her faith in God because this thing had happened to her. No good and kind Being such as the Christians preach about would have struck her in the back like this, said she. Therefore from henceforward she would wend her own way alone, without so much as an upward glance. Foolish, would-be-brave soul! Her heart was aching and she was distracted by the pain of the moment. She did not see that her argument against the existence of God was based on her personal experience and not on any form of reasoning that could be admitted. Had she reasoned out that God did not love mankind because typhoid fever was present in the world, she would have renounced her faith long before. Thousands of other people had died of typhoid fever, and it had not affected this good lady in the least. It was only when it struck home to her personally that she thought she must "curse God, and die."

Therefore, remember that your agony is part of a world filled with suffering. Remember that Jesus upon the cross entered into that sacred fellowship of pain and heartache which binds men everywhere into one great company. As a man once remarked

to his friend concerning his son who had recently
been killed, "If I had lost my son and God had not
lost his, I should have had a depth of experience denied even to God himself." But you know and I
know that this depth of experience has not been
denied to God, and that He takes us weary folks
in his arms with infinite tenderness, saying, "I know
the depth of your affliction because I, too, have suffered." When life tumbles in, the cross reminds us
that God has been all the way before us.

II

Nor should we forget that the untoward moments of life are but a part of the whole picture.
They loom large in our thinking because of the intensity of their emotional effect upon us, but their
reality is no more assured than many similar instances of happiness. Jesus hanging upon the cross
was stripped of everything except his eternal belief in the goodness and beauty and worth-while-
ness of things with which he had to do. He was
devoid of all happiness at the moment; he was be-
reft of his friends and his followers; he was cast
into the very depths of physical torture; and yet
he refused to say that the end of the world had
come because this thing had happened to him. His
was no petty outlook; his was a conception of life
that was large enough to encompass every event,
not merely the catastrophes. Driven from all se-

curity, he yet had faith in the hiding places of God, and was not afraid to trust them.

Let us disabuse our minds of the conception that there is nothing worse than pain or unhappiness or fear or bereavement. There are conditions of life which surpass these in possibilities for evil to us. Perhaps we do not win the victory we so earnestly seek at the particular moment that we think we should. Perhaps our souls are cast down because of a physical disability or a circumstantial handicap. That is not the whole of the picture, and we do ourselves and God wrong when we concentrate too intently upon such things.

In the summer of 1889 the Waldensians of Italy celebrated the return of the nation from exile some two hundred years before. They gathered in a narrow pass in the mountains of Piedmont to thank God for all that he had done for them. Two and a half centuries before this celebration the pope had dispatched an army of ten thousand men to massacre these Protestant people. The attack was not expected, and the people had not time to prepare an adequate resistance to the papal forces. There was but one thing that they could do. In that mountain pass there was a narrow path where only two men could march abreast. Six stalwart mountaineers said good-by to their families and went down there and held that pass against ten thousand men until their countrymen had a chance to escape, and they themselves were slain.

There was no great victory won in that mountain pass. The valleys were wet with blood, and the peaks of the mountains cried aloud the names of six men who had given their lives for the sake of those whom they loved. Suffering had been theirs, and suffering was the lot of their families who were bereaved of them. But that was not the whole of the story, and the little band who gathered two centuries later to pay honor to the memory of their ancestors remembered with grateful hearts that they were afforded this opportunity because of the suffering through which six men had passed. In defeat God had helped them as surely as in victory. It is a lesson as old as time itself.

There is one solid reliable truth with which all of us need to grapple at times: the sufferings of life are ultimately not the thing that matters nearly so much as the issues that come forth. Some men become cynical or morose when whips of suffering burn into their flesh; others lay hold upon things that have a long-range viewpoint, and win through to victory. Each man who succumbs to the inevitable, and is drowned by its incoming tides, has been lost to the world's good. But for each man who is able "to take arms against a sea of troubles" there will come a beauty of life that will send the rays of its inspiration far afield. This is the sort of thing that mankind has held up as its ideal, even though refusing to admit it. Heroism is not to avoid the danger; it is to accept it and bear it. Bravery is not to run whining to a hole in the wall; it is to stand firmly against the onslaught of the wind and the rain, and somehow make the stars to shine through the darkness round about.

I like that phrase that comes to us from the motion-picture world, "a star is born." It is not without its reality in the more prosaic world with which we have to do. Stars are born every day, without the fanfare and publicity that attends the development of some beauty-contest winner. Stars are born whenever men are too valiant to be crushed, too generous to be vengeful, too godlike to be scourged at night to some dungeon. Stars born this way shine with appeal that lights the steps of many another weary traveler. On every hand there are those who lift their faces to them and find ability to go on for another grueling day in the light of the stars.

Out of it all there comes one crystal-clear truth. For those of us who have been forced to bear with the stern reality of suffering, there is an eternal necessity that we learn the secret of the long way round. A straight line may be the shortest distance between two points, but it is not always the best distance. When God brought the Children of Israel up out of the land of Egypt they were as motley a group of ungovernable people as the world has ever seen assembled together. They had been under the hand of the Pharaohs for so many generations that they had no conception of the tremen-

THE CROSS AND GREAT LIVING

dous responsibilities involved in setting up a government for themselves. They needed to learn a
great many lessons, and there was but one way they
could learn them. As hard and crude as it may
have seemed to them, they wandered back and forth
within sight of the promised land for forty years in
order that their souls might find their capacities and
discover their limitations. Then when they went
into Canaan they were prepared for its struggles
and its joys. God knows what he is doing when he
keeps men wandering through the desert; he is testing their abilities to enjoy the oases which his eternal providences have prepared for them. The goals
do not change, only the path that leads to them
winds hither and thither through the fields of life.

Dr. Hutton, in the *British Weekly*, tells of the
caddies on the golf course at St. Andrews. He says
that these youngsters are more or less dictators in
their own sphere. Your caddy will hand you the
club, point the direction, remind you of the distance, and then stand back with folded arms to wait
the event. On one occasion a stranger was playing
the course, and not being accustomed to the type of
tyranny which was being exercised over him, was
somewhat disturbed by it. Finally they came to a
dog-leg hole which could be reached only by a cir-
cuitous route. The caddy handed him a club and
said, "You play on that black-roofed building over
there on the left." "Would it not be better," said
the stranger, "to go straight for the hole?" To

which the caddy replied, "You may play in any direction you wish. I was only suggesting how to play in order to win the hole."

We have our instructions! We can play this game of life any way we wish, but if we want to win we must play it the long way round. Sometimes it seems a foolish waste of time; sometimes it seems unbearable; but always there is the figure of that patient Man upon the cross. He too chose the long way, deliberately, and he watched every dream that a young man might have crumble into nothingness. He had no triumph heaped upon him because of his genius. One by one his brothers and sisters forsook him. One by one his friends left, to walk with him no more. When he needed them most his closest followers melted away in the darkness of his dying. But he never turned his head, never doubted, never stopped going steadily toward his appointed goal, and one day a million rainbows burst through the world's darkness because this Man had lived and died. He beckons us to follow this long, twisted, tortuous road that leads off into the distance where the horizons are hidden in the heart of the Creator God, and his spires rim the world. Can we? Will we?

THE CROSS AND CERTAINTY

*Jesus saith unto him, I am the way, the truth,
and the life.*—John 14:6.

IT IS A STRANGE, SEEKING AGE INTO WHICH WE HAVE
been born. It is an age in which values have been
overturned, ideals have been upset, hopes have been
smashed, and faith has been strained to the breaking point. Things in which men had found hope
and comfort for centuries suddenly have become
apparently lifeless before the onslaught of materialistic conceptions. We have seen things occur that
shall make our generation rememberable for centuries to come. Harsh and crass philosophies have
risen among us, and some have accepted them as
the only possible way out of world-wide catastrophe.

With it all there is but one thing men seek. We
have disguised it under a number of titles, but ultimately it is resolvable into one word—certainty.
We have called it "economic necessity" and have
suggested ways and means of providing pensions
and social security—and in another era "a chicken
in every pot and a car in every garage." It is all
merely a desire for certainty in our living. We
are anxious to know what things abide, what things
may be relied upon, what things will be the same

yesterday, today, and forever. Having discovered these, we feel that we shall be able to walk round the boulders that threateningly hinder our progress.

It is a tremendous step to say that the cross is the essence of certainty. That is an experience that none seeks, and all avoid if possible. But the Christian conception of the cross finds its explanation not in the event, but in the personality of Him who suffered thereupon. Two thieves died with the Galilean, but neither of them made an impression on the world. Hundreds of men were cast into the insatiable maw of the cruelty of Rome, but only One caused the cross to be set up as a symbol of triumph. The central fact of the crucifixion is that Jesus, the Christ, hung there. Out of that fact comes the certainty for which we are seeking. For the cross was the seal upon his living! Without this death he would have been but one more wise man who had walked among his fellows for a while, and then lain down wrapped in the arms of eternal sleep. But the crucifixion raised the man from the level of everyday, and set the stamp of the approval of God upon his work. Out of the things that he said we may weave a tapestry of truth, knowing that certainty in regard to these things is our right.

Among these sayings there is none with more significant meaning than, "I am the way, the truth, and the life." For him who would discover the foundation of rock on which to build his life, here is the answer. Certainty in regard to the changing experience through which we pass is guaranteed through this promise of Christ.

I

The Way may also be expressed as Ultimate Practicality. Life has its moments of romance, its times of daydreaming, its periods of wishful thinking. But it has also much that demands a practical solution of problems that stare us in the face. There is a picture by Alma-Tadema entitled "A Reading from Homer." In the background is the distant sea. On a half-circle marble seat there is a young man leaning forward in the intensity of the moment, his face aglow with the genuine pleasure that comes to the true scholar appreciative of the niceties of expression found in Homer. Around him is a group of a few choice spirits who have settled themselves comfortably to listen to the deathless melody of line that flows from the lips of the reader. The loveliness of it all is insidious. One lad in the front of the picture lies with his chin cupped in his hand, drinking in the words, with a rapt expression on his face as though he were living in another world. It is a very pleasant scene, but it is not a very practical scene. Life cannot be spent in listening to honeyed phrases mouthed for us by some silver-tongued reader. There are hard and crushing moments when reading alone is not sufficient to meet the demands. There are times when we can no longer be the audience, but must take our share in the whole rush of human affairs.

We do need desperately some way that shall prove its practicality to us in the ordinary affairs of life. We have tried so many ways, and have discovered their inadequacy to meet the situations of life. We have tried law, and commerce, and invention, and new forms of government, and still have seen our dreams crumble and our ideals blasted by the impact of a nonunderstanding world. We are longing for some way that will lead us into the realm of safe, sane, and happy living. We are wearied with the uncertainties of life, with the lack of purpose that manifests itself in so much of that with which we have to do. Daringly, some are willing to try this Way which Jesus offers. Hopefully, some are beginning to see that the essence of practicality is wrapped in the phrases he proclaimed so vigorously.

Unfortunately, we have not seen the deepest meanings in the outline of the Christian religion. A few more hardy souls here and there have been able to penetrate to the core of our faith, but the majority have been willing to accept the gospel of Christ as a mere adjunct to their living. They do not wish to do away with it, but it has never manifested any real power in their lives, either because they have been afraid to try its difficult demands, or they have never been convinced that his idealisms would really work in a world like this one. Religion is considered with a sort of inherited respect, but power is lacking because men are not willing to admit that the things Jesus said are possible of fulfillment. There has been no abiding conviction that religion is the persuasive power of a sovereign Spirit who speaks with the authority of the Divine.

So long as men conceive religion to be something set apart from their ordinary pursuits we need not expect great results from its ministrations. For those men who feel that the church is merely a place for their children to have Sunday school opportunities, where their wives can go on Sunday, and they themselves appear at Easter or now and again as honorary pallbearers at the funeral of a friend, we can promise no power. For such men are not willing to abide by the demands laid upon one who embraces our faith. They do not feel the stirrings of its deepest meanings. They are concerned with that which they call the practical part of living. But they neglect that which is most practical of all—the possibilities that are always present for him who knows the secret of Christianity.

The world has consistently torn down; just as consistently the religion of Christ has built up. Compare the ancient world, into which the Master came, with its utter disregard of human life, its contempt for all things ennobling, its disbelief in any future life, with our world today. Admitting the retrogression of our present age, there is a vast difference between our world and that of Christ. His religion has shown us the way. To dismiss his teaching with contemptuous shrugs of the shoulders, as though he had been an impractical idealist, is to admit one's ignorance of the workings of civilization. Apart from religion, a great deal of that in which we have been engaged has proved completely unproductive of happiness. Would it not be the part of wisdom, now, to try the Way? He is the only practical idea we have left.

II

The Master tells us further that he is the Truth, or Ultimate Reality. There is abroad an idea that only the material is real, that when we deal with those things that are unseen we have crossed the boundary line of reality. More careful consideration of such thinking readily proves its inadequacy. Material things have also their mysteries, which we are not able to penetrate, while spiritual things have their obvious realities. To deny either is to rob experience of its fullness.

Centuries ago, in a land of gold and spices, of luxury and happiness, whose "perfumes extended far out to sea," there ruled a queen named Balkis. Although possessed of all the material things that one could wish, she found her happiness bounded by her lack of knowledge as to the reason of things. Problems of the world vexed her; questions of eternity baffled her; and her spirit knew no peace. The look of inquiry which is born in the eyes of a child had grown to be a living question mark in the experience of this richly endowed queen. She was willing to undergo any experience necessary, if only she might learn the answers to her questions. Life and death were matters that concerned her, and she wanted to know the reasons behind the whole panorama of human existence.

But where could she find a philosopher wise enough to answer her questions? Then one day a courtier told her of a king named Solomon, who ruled in an obscure corner of the world, and whose reputation for wisdom had spread far and wide. The queen determined to visit him, and set about making her plans. It was no small undertaking, for it involved a journey of some fifteen hundred miles, over dangerous and unfamiliar territory. But no amount of hardship could turn this queen aside, for she was longing to come face to face with reality, and she had good hopes that this famous king could soothe her troubled mind with his words of wisdom.

In due time she arrived at his court with her very great train. Treasure sacks were opened, and gold and spices and rare Oriental commodities were showered as gifts upon her host. She gave Solomon ten thousand talents of silver, and no doubt he responded with a commensurate gift. Bows and courtesies were exchanged as the two rulers vied to impress each other with magnificence.

But the queen had not made this difficult journey merely to exchange gifts with another monarch. There is a legend that she fell in love with the man, and a son was born of their union. Be that as it may, we know that she was in love with the genius of the man, for had she not come a great distance to seek out the recesses of his mind, and to stand warmed by the sparkling radiance of his mentality? She wanted to know things, and this man knew the answers. Her curious, seeking mind was matched by his scintillating brilliance.

We wonder what questions throbbed upon her lips! Did she seek knowledge in the realm of science? He was the foremost scientist of his day, familiar with the habits of birds and beasts and and creeping things, with trees "from the cedar that is in Lebanon even unto the hyssop that springeth out of the wall." Did she seek understanding in literature? He was the most prolific writer of his day, speaking, according to his own record, "three thousand proverbs: and his songs were a thousand and five." His poetry has stood the test of time, and men still go to the poems of Solomon to learn the ways of language. Perhaps she questioned him in regard to matters of industry and commerce. He knew these things also, for he was the leading merchant of his day, with ships plying between Tyre and Ophir, and even distant Spain. In his business life he dealt in "gold, and silver, ivory, and apes, and peacocks." His shipyards at Ezion-geber were the marvel of his day. Perhaps she questioned him concerning the problems of state. Here again he had ready answers for her. His alliances with Egypt and Syrophoenicia were masterpieces of diplomacy. His country was well protected by chains of fortresses and a standing army of fourteen hundred chariots and twelve thousand cavalry, besides a large number of footmen. The internal condition of his land was good, with public improvements on every hand. Taxes were high, but the ruler was wise in his use of them, and the people were happy. Or did she ask him theological questions? Here, too, he knew the conventional answers, for he was the outstanding theologian of his day. He had built a temple and dedicated it himself. He could discourse learnedly on the nature and being of God. He knew the philosophies current in his age and the refutation of them.

But suppose she asked him about practical religion. Suppose she discussed with him the concepts of sin and duty, or character and destiny. Here he had nothing to say, for to Solomon all was "vanity of vanities." He knew only the things of the world, and ultimate realities were never his. So perhaps the queen returned to her own country disillusioned somewhat that a man could be so amazingly clever in a number of realms and so lacking in understanding in others.

A thousand years went by and a Man stood on the Porch of Solomon in the temple and cried out,

THE CROSS AND CERTAINTY

"I am the way, the truth, and the life." Those who listened knew that in him was that ultimate reality for which all hearts restlessly seek. He is the answer to the questions that well up in our hearts today, for he has shown us his understanding, and revealed to us his truth. Stretched mercilessly upon the cross, his lips still murmured, "I am the Truth." The centuries that have gone since that eventful day are witness that he was not mistaken.

III

In the third place, Jesus says, "I am the Life," or Ultimate Desirability. Here is the thing for which all of us are seeking.

> 'T is life, whereof our nerves are scant,
> O life, not death, for which we pant;
> More life, and fuller, that I want.

Beyond doubt, a part of that which Jesus meant in this phrase has to do with that which is popularly called "eternal life." But I am loath to separate the two. We live now; the experience shall be continued in a different form, and a different habitat, when we have shuffled off this mortal coil. Life does not end at a particular time. Jesus was constantly reminding his disciples that this experience is one with that which shall be. The abundant life of which the Master spoke so often is not confined to some shadowy abode of tomorrow. It is an actuality, here and now.

When this thought becomes real to us, it may serve to remove some of the pettiness from our living. Constricting our lives, because of our attempts to fill them to the brim with the pleasures of our generation, we have lost our ability to look at the stars; we have forgotten that we were not born to die, but to be heirs with God, and joint heirs with Jesus Christ. It is so easy to lose the spontaneity of our minds and hearts, because we immerse them so thoroughly in the ordinary pursuits of the day. We have become tied to the regulations of life, instead of being freed by them. "Life abundant" has become a phrase from the New Testament instead of shining truth to be used. Some years ago A. Edward Newton, writing in the *Atlantic Monthly*, said with gentle wit, "But for the unimpeachable integrity of Charles Lamb, we might well doubt his observation that lawyers were children once." The thought is worth pondering by each of us. We all have allowed ourselves at times to become mired in the laws of the world, instead of finding in and through them the abundant life that is possible to those who know where to seek it. Sometimes our thinking has become dusty and unfruitful; we have forgotten that we were children once, that life was big and rich and full of promise at that time. To lose that quality of expectancy, which is forever the portion of childhood, is to rob our living of something that has eternal value.

The life that Jesus offers us brings possibilities for everyday that are unlimited in their horizons. The tasks of the world constrict us by their ready limitations, but "abundant life" opens doors that lead out into the future, where the trails wind endlessly into the distance, and where the horizons of God beckon. We may live in time but we have eternity in our hearts. Carlyle's observation, "He who has no vision of eternity has no hold upon time," demonstrates its truth.

How do we know? There is a story from the Old Testament that shows us the light. It comes from the Book of Judges. One day a man named Manoah and his wife passed through a tremendous experience, and he was afraid for the future. "We shall surely die," he said, "because we have seen God." Let us not dismiss the idea as being a crude relic of anthropomorphism, with no place in our well-ordered scientific thinking. Expressed as it is, the thought is fundamental to life. Something had happened to this man that was too good to be true! He was afraid that he could not live with this amazing thing in his life!

His wife was one of those calm and profound persons whose insight into the ways of life is accentuated by their ability to express their thoughts in understandable terms. In her simple, meaningful way she said, "If the Lord were pleased to kill us, he would not have received a burnt offering and a meat offering at our hands, neither would he have shewed us all these things, nor would as at this time have told us such things as these." In other words, she is saying, "Do you think that God would lure us on with beauty and truth and faith and love and hope, and then, after giving us a glimpse of these things, kill us? It is not a reasonable speculation." Her insight is beyond refutation! We who know the Christ can understand her reasoning more perfectly, for in him is life, and this life is the light of men. We are confident that in him and his ways God has seen fit to reveal himself to us. It is an earnest of that which we shall know.

In his old age a man sat down to write a letter to some friends of his who were disturbed mightily because of world conditions and because of the difficulty of holding fast to things in which they believed. On every hand could be heard the thunder of hatreds, and there could be seen the clouds of misunderstanding of the Christian message. The fires of persecution already were being fanned by imperial direction. The old man, seeking for something to bolster their tottering faith, penned these words: "Beloved, now are we the sons of God, and it doth not yet appear what we shall be: but we know that, when he shall appear, we shall be like him; for we shall see him as he is." No higher ambition stirs our hearts today than that we might be like him. For we know, and are fully persuaded, that forever he only is "the way, the truth, and the life."

THE CROSS AND DOUBT

My God, why hast thou forsaken me?—Matt.
27:46.

THE WORD DOUBT CARRIES WITH IT A SINISTER
connotation. If we doubt the word of a man we
are, in effect, calling him a liar. If we doubt the
sincerity of his actions we are imputing to him a
deep-seated dishonesty. If we mention doubt as
regards our religious impressions we are assailed
as destroyers of the faith, and the body of the
church looks askance at our questing efforts to
discover truth. There are certain things that have
been looked upon as inviolable, and not to be questioned in any way. The church has called the
doubter a wicked man, and, in some instances, has
placed him under the ban for no greater reason
than that he doubted some things he could not
prove to his own satisfaction.

Like much of our living, it is a misplaced em-
phasis to deny the inherent good there may be in
honest doubting. Tennyson sings:

> There lives more faith in honest doubt,
> Believe me, than in half the creeds.

A more modern poet, Philip James Bailey, expresses
it:

Who never doubted never half believed;
Where doubt, there truth is,—'tis her shadow.

Certainly Jesus did not condemn the man who
doubted, provided he remained open to conviction.
Jesus chose one such to be with him, and made
him a disciple. Thomas was always stubbornly
loyal to his Master, but he feared to believe too
much, lest the subsequent disappointment be dis-
astrous to him. Only swelling tides of conviction
were able to keep his beliefs afloat.

Not only did Jesus fail to condemn doubt; the
fourth word from the cross carries with it an im-
plication that the Master himself at the moment was
torn with doubt as to the existence of God in his
own life. Readily admitting that his state of mind
on the cross was essentially different from his habit-
ual mood, we must face the fact that the Master
of us all was caught in the meshes of wondering if
God still cared for him, if the One whom he had
called Father had left him alone in his moment of
despair. It was for Jesus the blackest moment of
all his experience, for in the past he had been continually buoyed up by the assurance of the presence of God. Now, for the time, even that was
gone, and it seemed to this heartbroken man that
he faced the agonizing ordeal alone. From his
heart was wrung a cry that symbolized his affliction, "My God, my God, why hast thou forsaken
me?"

In our world where religion is so often considered as a varnish or a wishful dream; where open skepticism mingles with hidden ridicule; where men have watched that which they thought was marble turn to mud before their eyes; in a world like this, besieged and harassed and perplexed with doubts of a thousand sorts, we have every reason to remember the Strange Man upon a cross who lifted his bloodstained, tear-washed face to heaven to cry, "Surely not you, God. If all others go, I must still have you! Where are you, Father God?" In his agony we find our peace. Here at the cross are the answers to our questions.

I

Certainly this doubt which may have crossed the mind of Jesus was not that of ignorance. There must be a basis for belief or it cannot stand at all. We must have knowledge of the possibilities that are inherent in a situation or we cannot intelligently doubt them. Much of our misunderstanding of the principles of religion arises from ignorance of those principles. Admittedly we are lost in forests of darkness at times, but suppose we stop to take our bearings by making sure what all the trees round us mean. We have been ready to deny everything that smacks of the supernatural, without going through the arduous task of finding out what it is we are discarding. Various doctrines of the church have been under fire by those who do not have a clear conception of that which these doctrines really teach. The existence of God, the immanence of the Creator, divine Providence, and other supernatural events and affairs have undergone drastic denial on the part of some who were not sure just what they were refuting. God is not to be found in the hole of a groundhog! He who has the temerity to deny God should be quite sure of the grounds on which he bases such denial.

The future is hidden from us. We must be faithful to our ignorance of tomorrow, for we have no alternative. None knows the results of tomorrow's living, for tomorrow is yet to be born. Most of us have come to realize that did we know the events of the future, life would become desperately prosaic. The thrill of living lies in the unknown future. If we were to know it all, then science would be finished and the tools could be laid aside. No more wondering, for everything would be in plain sight. What a prosy and unhappy existence that would be for humans whose nerves are attuned to high adventure. As a modern writer points out:

No more delicious torture of being in love, no more exquisite pain of wondering if she will say "yes" or "no": it is eugenically plain and fixed what she will say! No more heaven to be gained, no more mystery in the Godhead: all roads are charted, and there are upholstered busses with free wheeling to transport us! No more hope! For (has it occurred to us?) if hope is killed when we say, "It is not possible," hope is just as dead when we say, "It is all discovered." [1]

Since these things are true, it behooves us to be sure that our ignorance is not more widespread than necessary. It becomes an obligation of our intellectual honesty that we be sure that which we deny has a reason for its denial. It devolves upon our religious experience to search out a matter as expertly as possible before saying, "I do not believe."

Again, we note that this shadow of doubt that crossed the mind of the Master was not due to prejudice. There are some unfortunate persons who have made a decision not to believe anything unless they are forced to. Their search for truth becomes in reality a search for an argument. Their motto apparently is, "What is better than seeking truth?" forgetting that the ready answer is, "Finding truth is forever better than seeking it."

Joseph Fort Newton reminds us of the painting by Watts entitled "Hope." A woman is sitting on the globe of the world with a harp in her hand. Above and beyond in a dark night sky there is but one tiny star which dimly shines. But the woman is not looking at the star. She is not looking at anything, because she is blindfolded. And every string on her harp, save one, is broken. Yet she sits poised, her hand eager to strike that string, confident that light will shine and music will sound.

[1] George A. Buttrick, *The Christian Fact and Modern Doubt*, Charles Scribner's Sons, 1934, p. 284.

It is a good picture to show such an age as ours.

Those whose prejudices have so arranged their thinking that they are clouded over with doubt could find little consolation in such a scene. Prejudice against belief destroys hope, in that it does not allow the entrance of light. It effectively plugs every gap through which truth and hope might shine to light the way of men. It is a foolish way to face the problem of living. Jesus had small patience with men and women who came to him expecting him to rearrange their prejudices for them. Earnest seeking after truth he was always ready to further, but captiousness he could not abide. If a man wished to find God, Jesus was willing to spend half the night with him—as he did in helping Nicodemus penetrate the darkness of his religious experience—pointing out paths down which the questing mind might run. But honesty in the search Jesus demanded.

The scales of belief are delicately balanced. The attitude of each individual determines which way those scales shall tip for him. To determine not to believe, because it is sometimes difficult to understand, is to spurn the privileges offered by human faith. To him who says that Democritus, the Greek philosopher, did not believe, we reply that Plato, who was a greater philosopher, did believe. If John Dewey is cited as an unbeliever, William James, who is not less eminent in intellectual achievements, may be adduced as a believer. If

Aldous Huxley is suggested as a religious skeptic, Robert Millikan may be pointed to as a scientist who accepts Christianity as the essence of truth.

It is well to remember the moment of doubt which assailed the Master on the cross. It helps in our own living to be reminded that Jesus himself once wondered if God still cared for him. But with such thoughts we must always remember that the feeling which Jesus had was an "honest doubt" and not a "dishonest prejudice."

Yet once more, we are confident that whatever doubt may have caused Jesus to cry out, "My God, why hast thou forsaken me?" was not based on indifference to truth. In every age there are those who find it difficult to believe. But so long as this difficulty is vibrant in living, concern for them need not be overwhelming. Men and women who seek truth with sincerity of purpose come to know God.

One of the most disturbing facts of our modern living is that men are not concerned about their unbelief. They are not sufficiently moved by it to investigate the possibilities of faith in the Unseen. That they have lost God entirely does not give them pause at all. This tragic happening cannot fail to have far-reaching consequences in the corporate life of humanity.

In order to avoid these results men of today must give themselves more assiduously to forms of meditation. An intelligent being should not simply accept that which is told him without making some

135

effort to verify it and have it prove its validity. Life is more than a mere round of sweeping rooms, managing offices, and worrying over the bills that come due with such astonishing regularity. Life is full and big with possibilities for understanding. He who simply doubts it all in an indifferent sort of way is wasting his heritage as a man. That a belief in God still remains essential to an adequate appraisal of human values is the measured judgment of the majority of men. Those who have put him out of their lives would do well to examine their hearts fairly to discover if they can live fully without him.

There is a legend telling of the day when men first began to feel a kinship with the gods, that day when they dared to walk a little more proudly across the face of the earth because they felt a sense of oneness with the supernatural. But the gods were jealous, and they stole away that spark of their own life. Then came the perplexing question where they might hide it so that man would not find it again. Weeks and months passed and their search was to no avail. Man ranged the mountains and plumbed the depths of the seas and peered inquiringly into the heavens. Wherever the spark was put man found it sooner or later. At last the great god Brahm took the spark in his hands and vanished briefly from the council chamber of the gods. When he returned, with a smile on his face, he announced, "I have hidden the spark

safely in a place where man will never look for it.
I have hidden it securely in his own heart."

Such an indictment is too true to be comfortable!
Let no doubts that arise in our hearts be the product
of a cold indifference to truth. Such is a too tragic
denial of our birthright.

II

Let us turn to the positive side of the doubt that
shadowed the soul of the Master. Why did he
doubt? Well, partly it was based on physical
agony. Jesus had, by the time these words were
spoken, been for a considerable period on the cross,
and with each passing moment the torture became
more unendurable. The wounds in his hands and
feet, exposed to the sun, grew baked and hardened;
the blood, prevented from following its normal
course through the body, swelled in heart and brain.
To move from one intolerable position to another
sent messengers of pain along every tingling nerve.
When men are passing through physical pain such
as this, their minds are distorted and their vision
is befogged. Even the face of God recedes into
the distance, or becomes a mask of terror from
which to fall back.

This sort of thing has happened in the lives of
so many of us, and it seems scarcely a kindness to
recall memories that burn themselves into our flesh
by the mere act of bringing them to mind again.
There are some things that we wish we could forget

forever; among them are recollections of storm-tossed days and sleepless nights of pain. Surely there can be no great virtue in recalling such experiences. The art of forgetting is something that all of us must cultivate at times.

But we cannot escape the fact that pain is woven into the texture of human life in such a manner that we cannot escape its ravages. We shall not enter into a discussion of its place in the scheme of things, but merely point out a practical rule for meeting such untoward moments. When pain sweeps in like a mighty tide to engulf our defenseless heads, let us concentrate hard on the positive side of our faith. Then it is much more difficult to keep firm hold upon things that are eternal. Like fires of hell, pain tortures our frail bodies without deliverance, and we groan and travail together in the agony of the moment. Doubt as to the goodness of God raises its ugly head, and we are powerless to escape its attack. Jesus knew what this meant, and desperately he clung to the things that he did believe. He won through to a quiet confidence in the midst of his physical suffering.

When pain strikes, the mind is not in fit condition to grapple with the problems that are presented. A much more excellent way is to know whom you have believed in calmer moments, and to be fully persuaded that he is able to keep that which you have committed to him. Doubts may not be dispelled entirely, but they will be held in abeyance until more rational moments have come—when the pain is gone and the dawn brings light.

But not all of Jesus' doubt was born of physical pain. There was mixed with his suffering an effort on his part to raise his spirit to God, and in the blackness of the moment it seemed an impossible task. In other words, some of the doubt through which Jesus passed was caused by intellectual difficulty. There are crises when it seems that the world is out of joint and nothing goes right. There are moments when it seems that the reins have slipped from the hands of God and the chariots of life are plunging heedlessly, recklessly toward disaster. We cry aloud at the injustice of the world, or the unfairness of life's experiences, or the apparent abandon of the principles on which civilization is built, the continued crucifixion of right and the enthronement of evil. It is all very difficult to understand and explain. If God exists, then "Why these things?" is a very logical question at times.

Let us suggest two things as possible techniques for facing our moments of intellectual doubting. First, let us admit that Christianity contradicts no known fact of human knowledge. At no place can one demonstrate a logical falsity in our faith. The point at issue is that men are asked to believe something outside themselves, which they could not find out for themselves, but only through some process of revelation. Sometimes this pierces deeply within our supposed armor of self-sufficiency. Milton represents Satan as falling from heaven because of pride. It is a parable of existence. We must remember that the mind of Jesus was not less brilliant than our modern thinking, and normally he found a satisfaction in God that was overwhelming in its intensity.

The other thing that we must do in regard to these intellectual difficulties is to change our conception of them. We have tried to hide our doubts under the bushels of conventionalities. We have been a little ashamed that we could not believe just as everybody else seemed to believe. After all, each of us is seeking truth. If doubts assail, there is no reason for us to attempt to dismiss them unsolved, as though we were committing some dreadful sin in having them flash across our minds. Like a rapier flashing in the light, the mind of man should dart hither and thither seeking truth only. Not all the questions will be answered, but honest seeking enables one to choose some "if" when certainty becomes impossible. It is forever better to love truth more than a lie, and the man who has honest doubts is a seeker after truth. But remember, only God knows all the answers. Do not doubt a thing simply because you cannot understand it. Leave to him some measure of intelligence beyond ours.

The late Francis G. Peabody, after a visit to the Orient, told the students at Harvard:

I was once travelling in an Oriental country, where life was squalid, women despised, and houses built of mud; and of a sudden, I came upon a village where all seemed changed. The houses had gardens before them and curtains in their windows; the children did not beg of the passer-by, but called out a friendly greeting. What had happened? I was fifty miles from a Christian mission-station, and this mission had been there for precisely fifty years. Slowly and patiently the influence had radiated at the rate of a mile a year, so that one could now for a space of fifty miles across that barren land perceive the salt of the Christian spirit, and could see the light of the Christian life shining as from a lighthouse fifty miles away.[2]

Such is the most effective apology for our God and his Christ. Whenever doubts assail me I think once more of the things that have been done in the name of God, and I am well assured that the faith of millions of people could not be built upon sand.

Like you this Christianity or not?
It may be false, but will you wish it true?
Has it your vote to be so if it can?
Trust you an instinct silenced long ago
That will break silence and enjoin you love
What mortified philosophy is hoarse,
And all in vain, with bidding you despise?
If you desire faith—then you've faith enough:
What else seeks God—nay, what else seek ourselves?

[2] *Mornings in the College Chapel*, Houghton Mifflin Co., 1907, II, 53. Used by permission.

THE CROSS AND PRAYER

*And he was withdrawn from them about a stone's
cast, and kneeled down, and prayed.*—Luke 22:41.

FOR CENTURIES MEN HAVE ASKED THEMSELVES THIS
question, "What makes this strange Nazarene different from any other who has lived?" The fact
of the difference is not doubted, but the secret of
its existence is constantly sought after. Men approach him from different viewpoints, and their
titles for him are of different wording, but his
sovereignty is not seriously disputed. Music, art,
literature, all the nobler pursuits of mankind unite
in common voice to give precedence to this Man.
In him begin and end the things that make life
worth while, that underscore its deepest and most
significant meanings.

Wherein does this difference consist? He was an
ordinary Man who trudged the roads of life with
wearying feet, who taught his truth as occasion
offered, who proclaimed good tidings of great joy
to those who had ears to hear, who was finally
crushed by Roman despotism just as the flower of
his life was opening. Other men have done these
things, other men have died in some agonizing sacrifice for something in which they believed. Why
has this life projected itself into the centuries?

142

The disciples found the secret and sought to have him share it with them. "Lord, teach us to pray." For in that high communion with God was wrapped the spirit of Christ, and from it there flowed the rivers of living water that he was able to give unto others. Prayer was not an addendum to the life of Jesus—it was bread and meat. In the air and atmosphere of prayer he made his greatest decisions; with prayer he sealed his suffering into holy dying. Upon the wings of prayer his spirit soared across the realms of the temporal and dwelt with the eternal God. He who would share the secret of power which Jesus possessed must learn to pray.

At no time in the experience of the Master was prayer more urgently a part of his being than at the time of his passion. In the Garden of Gethsemane, and later upon the cross, prayer was the warp woven in with the woof of sacrifice that made the redemptive act possible. Without the sustaining courage of prayer he could not have walked the road that led down, down into a valley where the fires burned white hot, where his naked soul was seared with agony. Only his faith sustained him when every star in the heavens was blotted out, and that faith found its secret springs back in the hills where he had learned to pray. Three questions suggest themselves to us as we consider the prayer life of Jesus, exposed in the gleaming white light of Calvary.

I

The first of these questions is, "To Whom did Jesus pray when the winds of adversity were blowing bitterly about him? To Whom did he lift his voice when shame and suffering and humiliation swallowed him like a great net closing about his defenseless head?" The answer is not difficult to discover. Listen! "Father, if it be possible, let this cup pass from me." "O my Father, ... thy will be done." "Father, into thy hands I commend my spirit." Jesus was convinced that the God to whom he prayed was not some far-off force making for righteousness; not some principle of love or charity; not some law or power by which the universe was guided on its journeys through space; not some incarnation of energy, such as electricity or gravitation; but a Father—a warm, vibrant, conscious personality.

The implications of this thought are tremendous in their possibilities. Modern religion emasculates itself when it attempts to serve its interests in an ethical manner only. We cannot expect religion to be the mainstay of humanity in critical moments if all that we have is the thunder of Sinai or the denunciations of the prophets. We must also have the Cloud and the Pillar of Fire; we must also have the promises of the prophets; we must also have a *Being* who is as real as life itself. Otherwise our religion becomes philosophy and has no necessary place in the affairs of men. The man who attempts

144

to direct his prayers to an abstraction only will discover that his religious experience becomes thinner and thinner until there is no substance left— it is a mere sham. To remove the fact of a personal God from our thinking leaves little that is worthy of the name religion.

Fundamentally we must be honest with ourselves! We must not try to delude ourselves into believing something that is not there. By all means let us welcome every investigation that will turn the cold, impersonal searchlight of truth upon every assertion that we make. But correspondingly, let us be ready to accept the implications inherent in the efforts of some to destroy the personality of God. It is a subterfuge, out of which eventually will come the destruction of all the faith we have known. A skeptic of the last century writes feelingly of the loss sustained in his own life when he felt that the Great Companion was no longer with him. It is one of the deep-rooted urges of human nature. We do well to listen to its insistent voice.

As the years go by our questions concerning God become more complex, and more urgent in their demand for evaluation. Life at first is filled with a number of things, and we are swept before the flow of their tides. But as time marches on we discover that some of the things about which we had been so busy have lost their importance to us, and we are much more concerned with things unseen and eternal. We come to question the nature of God, not in a skeptical manner, but in an honest effort to discover the type of being God is. As we send our questing minds on these expeditions for truth, we are led to see that religious faith is rooted and grounded in the fact that God exists as we exist. Early in life it may seem that God does not matter; but later, when we realize that nothing matters but God, we want the sort of God to whom Jesus cried out, "Father, Father."

Ultimately, faith in prayer is dependent upon this fact alone. We will find cold comfort in lifting an agonized spirit to a principle or a force—it must be to a Father or we know the exercise is vain. Only then can we understand the nature of the answer that comes to our praying. Only then can we give our hearts and lives to him in the complete dedication that makes true prayer a golden chain about the feet of God. Only then does the same type of faith that Jesus had lay firm hold upon our hearts.

A farmer once heard a little orphan boy, who had never had much opportunity in life, repeating the letters of the alphabet over and over again, as he knelt on the hard, stony ground of a field near the farmer's house. "What are you doing, lad?" asked the farmer. "Please, sir, I'm praying," returned the child. "But, boy, that's not praying," said the man. "Yes, sir, I know it's not," said the boy. "But, you see, I don't know how to pray, and I heard the minister say that if a person talked to God he would know what that person needed most. I thought I would just say the alphabet and let God put the letters together into the kind of prayer that I would like to say."

Childish as it may seem, that is the sort of thing to which belief in the personality of God ultimately leads one. And in spite of our sophistication and lack of naïveté, we know that a trust like that will bring more real happiness than any other attitude we could assume. Jesus believed that his Father would never forsake him; consequently his life was radiant always.

II

Oftentimes hanging on the walls of offices of particularly devout men there is a little motto, embellished with flowers and scroll work, "Prayer Changes Things." Does prayer really change things, or is that simply wishful thinking on our part? It is a question that throbs for an answer, for our attitude toward prayer depends in large measure upon an adequate answer. In the life of the Master, we find that his prayer for escape from the rigors of the crucifixion did not provide an open door for him. The crucifixion was a necessary part of the plan of God for the salvation of the world, and he would not be swayed from that purpose, even by the prayers of his Son. Jesus knew that, and did not allow his human dread of the agonies involved in this experience to overshadow all his thinking. He was willing to place the entire affair in the hands of God, confident that whatever might be the outcome it would be according to the Father's will, and therefore for the best.

Does prayer work modern miracles of release from steel bands of suffering? Does prayer bring rain to drought-cursed areas? Does prayer make and break empires because one national group has been more diligent in seeking the favor of the Almighty? Such questions, and those of kindred nature, sharpen themselves upon the facts that we must acknowledge.

Let us honestly and freely admit that there are limits to this exercise of prayer. The poet sings, "More things are wrought by prayer than this world dreams of." With that sentiment we are in hearty accord; but, to be worth while, prayer must set and recognize its own limitations, and not attempt to go beyond them. To do so is to nullify the good that is inherent in the exercise. Obviously there must be limits to that which prayer can do in the natural world. If law and order were at the whim of ardent prayers it would be impossible for us to live at all. If prayer could so intoxicate the law of gravity that one day it pulled up, the next day down, and the third day exerted no influence at all, life could not continue. If a man should go to his office some morning and discover that the stairs had disappeared, and the roof was

148

on the ground, and the walls were leaning in various precarious positions, he could accomplish little work. Only because certain things are faithful are we able to live in the world.

In attempting to shift the channel of things because it suits our petty convenience, we do well to remember that the laws which we seek momentarily to annul are the basis of all the freedom we know. If we attempt to persuade the Creator to shift the rain to tomorrow because of our planned picnic for today, we are dabbling in affairs of the universe of which we have woefully inadequate understanding. Fortunately, God is not so easily moved. Mastery in living comes from using its handicaps, not by removing them whenever they become irksome. Football is a grand game because men have a goal bounded by certain limits, not because a man may run all over the city whenever he gets the ball. Prayer does not set aside the limits that a wise Providence has made the basis of our free existence.

But let this solving word be added. There are laws higher than the ones that we know. As prayer infuses our being it enables us, with courage and insight, to reach after things we had not dreamed possible before. Ships sail uphill in the locks of a canal; bodies heavier than air float safely and comfortably in the upper reaches of the sky; men live for days on the bottom of the ocean. No laws have been repealed, but men have discovered higher

149

laws. Who can compute the possibilities that are ours when we learn to think God's thoughts after him in true prayer?

Dr. Buttrick retells and comments upon an illuminating incident that happened some years ago. A Methodist minister in Stroudsburg, Pennsylvania, prayed that God would destroy the liquor traffic, and that he would begin the good work by striking the local brewery with lightning. The next day the requested thunderstorm appeared and the brewery was destroyed. The brewer heard about the prayer the minister had made, and sued him for damages. The county court dismissed the case. The brewer was among the faithful; the county court among the skeptics. But who was right? [1] Does prayer enter the minutiae of our living, and cause God to loose his thunderbolts at our insistence? To entertain the thought is to admit the chaos that would result from such cross-purpose praying as constantly goes on in our world. Prayer will have much more realistic value to us when we come to accept its obvious and necessary limits. In no sense are we thus limiting the Creator —he hears the prayers, but he does not grant them.

III

But is that little motto, "Prayer Changes Things," all wrong? By no means! He who says that

[1] *The Christian Fact and Modern Doubt*, p. 189; referring to *Church Management*, January, 1932.

prayer does not change things has simply not observed the course of human life. Prayer forever changes things because prayer changes people, and people are the masters of things. It is a shabby question to ask, "What good is prayer? What will I get out of it?" We do not ask a similar question of friendship, or of music, or of art, or of the beautiful things of nature. Whenever a man begins to point out that prayer has given him this or that, it is wise to avoid his religious inclinations. They are apt to lead one into an impasse. Jesus got a cross out of his praying. But that was not the important thing. The prayers of Jesus were the lever by which he was able to assume the weight of human redemption. They were the strength by which he carried the cross.

As someone suggests, if the only thing we are seeking from our prayers is some material benefit, then we had better cancel the whole program. God does not work with his children in such a manner. Mary Pickford's book a few years ago, *Why Not Try God?* no doubt was written with splendid intentions. But who are we that we should have the audacity to experiment with the Eternal, as one might keep a radio in his home for a week to see if the reception and tone were agreeable to his aesthetic tastes? The proposition must be reversed, and we must let God try us before we dare to hope that prayer will change things for us. Jesus proclaimed, above all else, that prayer is a communion between two kindred spirits—it is not a demand or a mental calisthenic. Oftentimes it does no more than link the spirit of man with that of his Creator; no answer is given to particular petitions. But can a human soul expect more than fellowship with God? Brave souls in every generation have discovered that this is the sunshine before which all tears are dried, all sorrows are melted.

Jesus would teach us, through his own praying, that a man must learn to give this entire scheme of living into the hands of God. The secret is not that we can *change* all things because we have asked God to perform the work for us, but that we can *do* all things that present themselves for the doing, through the power that prayer has brought to us. It becomes a new kind of power for changing things, because it stems from hearts that are changed. Flashes of insight and truth are given more and more frequently to the man who has come close to the heart of the Infinite. All in all, it is a staggering thought that we who live close to God can begin to feel, stirring in our breasts, the power of God himself. We can learn to think his thoughts after him, and to speak his language. This will not enable us to walk around the Calvaries of our experience. They will still face us, and we will still be called upon to walk the coals that are heated white hot. But we will have the strength and the courage to do so, if we have mastered the art of prayer. It is a goal not to be despised.

But power alone is not enough. Power in our world is confusing oftentimes, and we are afraid of its manifestations. An airplane has power—one hundred feet from wing tip to wing tip, weighing several tons, its mighty engines can hurl it through the air at a speed of two hundred miles an hour. But it is all controlled by the pilot who sits in the forward compartment. Power comes not merely from might, but from a mind able to control properly the manifestations of force that lie all about us. Power comes ultimately from the heart that is serene. So long as some Dr. Jekyll and Mr. Hyde complex ravishes our being we have no power, because we are torn between personalities. But when we have learned the secret of prayer, as Jesus knew it, then William James's fine expression becomes reality in our living, for we have "unified our divided selves."

The one thing most necessary in our world is calmness of heart and mind. We are distraught by the demands and complexities of civilization. It has not been essentially different with people of each generation, but this is the one with which we have to do personally. We must learn to bring our various desires and motives under a proper control, or serenity in living is impossible. As we are able gradually to focus these things in one direction, and have that direction never waver in its pointing toward God, we come to find that we are new creatures in Christ Jesus, and the former things have all passed away. Prayer focuses our wandering thoughts. Prayer develops new motives, refines old instincts, sharpens deep aspirations. There is much that God can and will do for us when we become ready to share his mind. Until we are thus receptive, even the hands of God are powerless to work for us.

What is prayer for? It is an answer to the deepest and most significant craving of the human heart. We do not seek in prayer some boon of earthly welfare alone; certainly we do not expect a mere mountain-removing magic. We seek the friendship of God, for, in the immortal phrase of Augustine, "our hearts are restless until they rest in God." Prayer is the bridge that leads the human heart from the world of everyday to the New Jerusalem of God, where the soul may fall prostrate before the ineffable vision of the glory of God, there to hear the angels saying, with the elders, "Holy, holy, holy, worthy art thou to receive the praise and the honor and the glory." And from such an experience we learn how Jesus drew his ability to say, "I have overcome the world." In prayer our cross becomes our crown, and a skeptical world pauses in awe, half understandingly, half wistfully, to say, "Behold, he prays!"

THE CROSS AND FEAR

Let not your heart . . . . be afraid.—John 14:27.

THERE IS ONE ASPECT OF LIFE WITH WHICH WE ALL have to do. We may delude ourselves in the comfort of some given moment that we are not afraid, that we never allow the clammy hand of fear to clutch our hearts, but really we know that we are just whistling in the dark, and that sometimes we are desperately afraid. There are so many things that threaten our safe living! There are so many things that are more powerful than we! There are so many things that we have not mastered in spite of our vaunted civilization!

Do you recall from a few years ago a delightful bit of the motion-picture art entitled *The Big Bad Wolf?* It was one of those animated cartoons called "Silly Symphonies"—an apt name, indeed! The story revolved around the wanderings of three fat and happy little pigs, and their efforts to escape their arch enemy, the big bad wolf. They had several narrow escapes, but did manage to get away each time, and celebrated their victories by joining hands and dancing to the tuneful melody, "Who's afraid of the big bad wolf? Tra, la, la, la, la." But the interesting part of the picture was that the moment the big bad wolf made an appearance the three little pigs scampered as fast as they could for whatever shelter was available. Their deeds belied their melodic bravery.

Because even nursery rhymes ultimately must find their meaning in human experience, we have in this simple amusement project a deep lesson of living. All men, as they face some big bad wolf, are afraid, and it is useless to regale the neighbors with superficial songs of bravery. We are afraid of life sometimes—it has been the common lot of humanity since time began. We may summon reserves of courage, but we are still afraid, and denial does not veneer fact. Adam was afraid when God called him; Moses was afraid when told to go to the court of the ruler of the world; Isaiah was afraid when commanded to become the mouthpiece of Jehovah; yes, even the Lord Jesus was afraid when he saw the cross looming before him. Had the Master failed to feel the heart-tightening, constricting emotion that we call fear, he would not have been human, and that would have made him an ineffectual Saviour. Fear was in his heart that night, just as it would have been in the heart of any one of us facing such an ordeal. But fear did not destroy him, because he knew how to use it. It need not destroy us if we know the same secret.

I

Let us, first of all, be very sure that the fears that stalk us like relentless beasts are real and not imag-

156

inary. Let us escape the idea that there is something wrong or repulsive about fear. The emotion means nothing in itself. A slight quickening of the heart action, an increase in the amount of adrenalin secreted in the blood system, a slight change in the percentage of sugar in the body—and we are afraid! But what difference should these things make? Chemical reactions are constantly taking place, causing one change after another in our bodies. What difference is it if these things do occur?

The answer seems to be, unequivocally, "None at all!" The emotion of fear is not to be shunned as though it were some plague about to descend upon us. Fear has a definite place in the life of each of us. The experience of personality would scarcely be possible without its component parts, and among them is fear. We are careful in crossing the street for *fear* we may be run down. A doctor is careful in making a diagnosis for *fear* that a mistake on his part will cost a human life. The sinner is restrained, the righteous worship, the brave act, each because *fear* is present and prompts each to a certain course of action. It is all a perfectly normal function of a human being.

Just as surely it is possible to fill our lives with imaginings which develop into destructive factors. We people the future with wild beasts of various sorts and then are constantly concerned lest we be attacked by them. In our calmer moments we see clearly enough that much of that over which we worry the most will, in all probability, not take place at all. But at the time we are plagued by the possibilities that face us.

It is foolish to attempt to dismiss this sort of fear as being a form of autosuggestion. Some have suggested that a man does not want to do something, and consequently his heart fails within him. The real reason, we are told, is not that the task is dangerous or onerous, but simply distasteful; therefore fear develops. It is an escape mechanism, and needs to be guarded carefully lest it keep us in fox holes of inaction when we should be up and doing.

But, as Dr. Buttrick points out,

In strict sense there is no autosuggestion, for whatever we propose to ourselves takes rise in some measure beyond ourselves. If in a dream we see our house attacked by green unicorns each with a tail like a meteor and eight legs shod with lightning, the dream would still draw for its material upon a world beyond ourselves. The combination may be ours, but not the ingredients: we have seen, in picture or in actuality, green, lightning, meteors, and unicorns. It is not in man's power, even in his thoughts, to make something out of nothing.[1]

As significant as that thought may prove, it must be admitted that we still make weird combinations of things we know, and green unicorns still march toward us in our dreams. We know that we are

[1] *Prayer*, Abingdon-Cokesbury Press, 1942, p. 49.

imagining these things, and yet they are so eternally difficult to root out of our thinking. All the things that may happen to us on the morrow press in on our spirits with devastating effect. We say that we will no longer consider them, but the will seems inadequate to cope with the situation. We find that we cannot roll up our sleeves, and grit the teeth, and say, "I will not be afraid." To do so often makes us act like the man who joined the Don't-Worry Club, and wrote a verse about his experience:

> I joined the new Don't-Worry Club
> And now I hold my breath—
> I'm so scared for fear I'll worry,
> That I'm worried most to death.

It is not a sufficient answer.

In order to meet fears of this sort we must do two things. First, we must indulge in a bit of analysis. In our hurried living there is not much time for introspection, and its loss is reflected in modern humanity. If we are afraid for the future, suppose we analyze the whole situation; and, lo! many times we discover that much of our fear is groundless. The future is uncertain, but God is in it. Love and patience and courage still have their tremendous appeal. It may be bad enough, surely, but still not as bad as we fear. That sort of attack will not rout all our fear, but it will eliminate a great many things that we dread.

The other thing we must do with our imaginary fears is to make an honest attempt to balance them with positive thoughts of courage. As we learn to do this we discover that fear retreats into the background while thoughts of our abilities as sons of God assume primary importance. It will not take place overnight, for this discipline comes only to those who are willing to sacrifice for it. But ultimately to the man who is anxious to counter-balance his fear of life there comes a way. It is long, sometimes, but the goal is sure.

II

We have been thinking of those things that harass us but have no basis in fact. Now let it be admitted freely that there are some things of which we are afraid which are as real as the clouds, as depressing as the rain, as destructive as the lightning. We do not well to hide our heads in sands of denial of these things.

G. K. Chesterton has a story of an architect with a supersensitive love of the beautiful. In the city of London, where this man lived, there was a very ugly house. The architect had seen it on one of his walks through the city, and was haunted by the fear that someday he might again be lured out for a walk and see that excruciatingly ugly house. Finally a brilliant idea was born in his mind—he would buy the house and live in it. So he did,

and never left it again. Consequently he never saw
it and was perfectly happy.

That may be one way to avoid the ugly things
of the world, but it is not a very sensible way.
Certainly it is not the Jesus way. The Master calls
us to go with him on his rounds through the world,
and freely admit that there is much which is distasteful, which is dangerous, which will destroy us
if we are not careful in our attitudes and actions.
There are some things of which we ought to be
afraid, and Jesus himself would admit their presence.

But the admission of them is scarcely enough.
What can be done about it? One great thing that
Jesus always does for men who commit their living
to him with a sense of moral earnestness is to take
them for a walk through the valleys of reality and
point out the hardships that are involved in his
way of life, and then say, "But you can do it if
you will trust enough. I did it, and my strength
belongs to you." What is the technique involved?

First, you must want to go on. The things of
which you are afraid may come to pass just as you
fear. They did in the life of the Master. All the
untoward, agonizing experiences that he dreaded
took place, and from no one of them did he find
escape. The furnaces were heated white hot, and
his body and soul were tried therein. But Jesus
kept going with irresistible courage, with undaunted
faith, with continued belief that the path he was
following would prove as richly rewarding as it

was, at the moment, difficult. Fear he must have known, for what body would not shrink from such an ordeal as that through which he passed? But above and beyond the fear there was a determination that he would not turn back, no matter what happened to him. Twenty centuries proclaim the wisdom of his outlook.

One of the brave men of Scotland's history is John Knox, the preacher. Woven of the same physical texture as you or I, there was implanted in his heart a fervor for righteousness that gave him no peace except as he crusaded for that in which he believed. On one occasion there was great rejoicing in the palace of Mary Queen of Scots. News had come across the channel that a great massacre of Protestants had taken place in France. Hundreds were dead as a result. Mary, the Catholic Queen, was so delighted that she gave a great party to celebrate the event.

The next Sunday the gaunt figure of Knox mounted the pulpit and denounced in measured phrases the rejoicings at the palace. He knew full well that this woman had the power of life and death over him, but seemingly he was unconcerned about that. Something had happened which did not fit into his scheme of the Kingdom of God on earth, and he publicly rebuked the guilty person.

Not many days passed before he was summoned to the presence of the Queen. The servants of Mary were deeply impressed by his bearing, and

162

the Queen was forced to admit that Knox was not a man to be intimidated. Fear he might have, but he had something more powerful than fear—he had the courage to go on in an appointed path no matter how afraid he might be. That sort of courage always comes to him who has an unconquerable conviction that the things for which he stands, or fights, are worth whatever sacrifice is called for.

Another thing we must learn, if we would be a conqueror and not a victim of fear, is that God is always with us. That is the deepest truth that Jesus left with humankind. If one forgets all else that he said, and remembers only that the Master promised, "I will not leave you comfortless: I will come to you," that person has the key to successful Christian living. We sometimes labor under the illusion that life ought always to be good to us, and that it has gone wrong if fear and worry and pain distract us. We mistakenly believe that God is with us only in our better moments and that we must bear the rest of it alone. Nothing could be further from the truth! Nothing could evidence a more complete lack of understanding of the nature of God!

Alfred Noyes wrote:

In the cool of the evening when the low sweet
    whispers waken,
  When the laborers turn them homeward, and the
    weary have their will,

163

When the censers of the roses o'er the forest aisles
   are shaken,
  Is it but the wind that cometh o'er the far, green
   hill? [2]

Or is it God? I like to think that it is! But
suppose it is all changed, and the cool of the evening
is the heat of noonday, when the weary are faced
with the dreary prospect of long hours of continued
weariness until exhaustion strikes them down, and
the censers of roses are bombs filled with poison
gas, while over it all there drone back and forth
the man-made engines of destruction that bring
death and despair to all below. What, then, about
this Unknown whom the poet professes to hear?

God is still there! The Voice still speaks! The
Strange Man still climbs green hills of human experience, though there may be again a cross upon
the summit. Wherever we go we can be assured
that He who became poor for our sakes will walk
with us. Afraid? Of course we are afraid at times;
we shudder at the prospect that lies ahead. But
we have a guaranteed Companion, and that enables
us to walk with utter confidence. There may be
fear, but there will be no spiritual collapse.

III

Since it is true that God walks with us in every
experience of life, it follows inevitably that the

[2] From "In the Cool of the Evening" in *Collected Poems*,
vol. I. Used by permission of J. B. Lippincott Co.

things of which we are most afraid often prove to be our greatest blessings in the sum total of our living. For the moment they are grotesque monsters threatening to destroy us, but their power is definitely limited, and in that limitation we find our hope. Fear produces something within the soul of a man that cleanses and purifies and brings him closer to the Infinite. That something falls out to his eternal advantage, for it is a stepping stone provided by no other method in living.

It is an interesting exercise to read the New Testament and discover the number of times that the emotion of fear is mentioned. Those men and women of the first century were afraid so often that it became a refrain of life. But constantly there was a Voice: "Be not afraid. Put your trust in God, and not in the things of the world." And, lo! some believed that there were possibilities in that sort of thing and they laid firm hold upon some aspect of faith, and though they were tried as by fire they did not let go. And these men and women won through to a complete peace. The things of which they had been the most afraid became the factors that produced the clearest understanding.

On the Judean hills were a group of shepherds. Suddenly the whole field of the sky was ablaze with glory, as an angelic choir sang an anthem never before heard in the world. Small wonder these shepherds were afraid, and wondered what heavenly visitation was theirs that night. But they followed the gleam, and around the cradle of the Babe of Bethlehem they found that their fear was a forerunner of their greatest joy.

One night the disciples were on the lake where they spent so many hours. The Master was not with them, for he had gone into the mountain to pray. During the evening the wind rose and the sea bared its teeth at those who dared to sail its bosom. But these men were accustomed to the tempests of the lake, and they were not afraid until they saw a white shape moving across the waters toward them. Then their blood turned to water and they cried aloud for fear. Like the notes of a clear-sounding bell there came a voice: "Be of good cheer; it is I; be not afraid." That of which they were afraid was the Man whom they loved and trusted.

Another night a group of the disciples was gathered in an upper room to celebrate the Feast of the Passover. There was a hint of danger in the furtive preparations they had made for the supper. There was an atmosphere of intrigue that had stifled them as they walked the crooked streets of Jerusalem during that day. They knew that this Man whom they followed was hated by the powerful interests of the city. They had watched him antagonize these men beyond endurance in the past several days by his calm insistence upon the principles of complete righteousness as compared with

166

their stupid evasions. The disciples were afraid, and their anxiety was reflected in every action. Then, like dew falling upon parched flowers up-turned to catch the moisture, came the words: "Let not your heart be troubled: Ye believe in God, believe also in me. . . . . Let not your heart be troubled, neither let it be afraid." It was not quite enough for them. Human like, they continued to be afraid throughout that horrible Friday and that desperate Saturday. But then came Easter Sunday, and the factors of which they had been so fearful combined to produce a resurrection.

It may not be possible to live without fear creeping into our hearts on its little cat feet. But it is possible to find Something so big that all else fades before it. Fear, then, cannot hide the light of courage, and the evening time becomes as day. Such is the gospel of Jesus Christ, and he who finds it is eternally wise.

THE CROSS AND POWER

And I, if I be lifted up from the earth, will draw all men unto me.—John 12:32.

FROM THE BEGINNING OF TIME MEN HAVE DESIRED power. Some have wanted only enough to meet circumstances that threatened the happinesses of everyday living. Others have longed for power to reach coveted goals of human achievement. Still others have had such an insistent urge within their hearts for complete authority over their fellow men that they have bathed their generations in blood in the satisfaction of this desire.

The history of the race has been an interesting trek from the mud and slime of prehistoric days, through the dawn of intelligence, into the full morning of life as we know it. In every age there have been those willing to sell their souls if thereby they were able to attain a greater degree of power. We of the twentieth century are not vastly different from men of the first century in this respect.

In the early days of human history the magnificence of the Pharaohs dwarfed all else before its splendor. Then mighty Babylon extended her sway through the reaches of the known world, and the names of her emperors were spoken with bated breath by men near and far. Rome appeared, gathering to herself more and more power, until her legions tramped the world and her navies bridged the seven seas. Then, later, the balance of power shifted to northern Europe, and the Holy Roman Empire decided the destinies of nations. Then France, then England, then Prussia—like some child's seesaw, back and forth, men seeking for power, holding it momentarily, and then being forced to relinquish it because they could not tame themselves, and were broken upon the racks of their own devices.

How utterly different is the power emanating from the Roman cross on which Jesus hung, as it stands sharply outlined against the blackness of human depravity that made it possible! Through centuries men have turned to this power, and have discovered that here is something unique among the power-filled things of the world. The cross is still the tallest mountain peak of them all. However difficult it may be to understand, however impossible it may seem to our logic-seeking minds, the fact remains that the cross has proved its power in the lives of millions of people. It towers over the wrecks of time because it has demonstrated its eternal worth and reality. We look back upon the vanished power of the Pharaohs and the Caesars, Sennacherib and Charlemagne, and, like Paul, stand upon the ashes of human power and wisdom, holding aloft the cross of Christ. Wherein consists its power?

I

Let us note that it is not the power of age. The cross, as an historical event, is one of the newcomers to the world. It happened a mere nineteen hundred years ago; and when we consider the age of our world, anything that happened so recently as that is not ancient in any sense. Further, the greatness of age could not be ascribed to the cross because it began to manifest its power within a score of years after the sacrifice of the Master was complete.

This is not to deny that there is certain power in age. China, today, is great in its own way, because it traces its civilization for four thousand years. But that power is definitely limited, and if China should be left to her own devices she would fall an easy prey to the ravages of Japan. Power of age often rests on a false basis, and does not allow sufficiently for the strength that may be inherent in human progress. The cross manifests its worth to humanity by its complete adaptability to every age and every demand that may be made.

Nor is the power of the cross that of circumstance. Occasionally things fall out in such a manner that undue power is given to one nation or another. For a while recently, Turkey was possessed of unusual power because both the United Nations and the Axis were anxious to have Turkey's resources fall as a prize into their laps. The Turkish government played its part most discerningly, and joined neither side. Here was circumstantial

170

power, coming to a nation from forces outside, with which the nation itself had, in reality, nothing to do. It is not a new or different sort of power; we see the same thing happening every day. Here is a man born wealthy—and who can deny the inherent power of wealth?—but the power is that of circumstance, in that it was thrust upon him through no effort of his own. Of course the use of the power is determined by the man himself, but with its creation he had nothing to do. This sort of power cannot be ascribed to the cross. Circumstances were such that they would have served to remove all power from this strange Galilean, rather than increase his might in the eyes and hearts of men.

Neither was the power of the cross that of raw might. How often we have seen this sort of power manifested in our world! How sickened we have become of the impact of mailed fists upon the doors of our safe and comfortable living! How foolish this type of power has proved itself in the long-range view of history! Yet how continually men believe that this sort of power will maintain their prized customs or open for them the treasure chests of the earth! It is false power in that it lasts only so long as the other man is weaker than his conqueror. Inevitably there comes a day when the tables are turned, and life becomes more complicated than ever.

In our world there are certain nations which

171

profess to believe that might is right. We believe that our mission is to eradicate that philosophy from the councils of men. But we must have a care that it does not pervade our own thinking. When victory comes we must maintain a real power, and not that of brute force. We must never forget that Japan is a group of islands out there in the Pacific, whose millions of inhabitants never have enough to eat and never maintain a standard of living comparable to our slum districts. If we think that the power of the brute is going to solve that sort of problem, we have failed to read the lessons of history aright. The cross can solve it, but then that power is not the "raw might" type.

Further, the power of the cross is not that of law. In the universe certain laws are unalterable. He who breaks them will find himself punished by them. But the working out of such processes is tedious and long, and we become wearied with waiting for the power of law to manifest itself. Dreadful times come when

> .... The sensuous frame
> Is rack'd with pangs that conquer trust;
> And time, a maniac scattering dust,
> And Life, a Fury slinging flame.

The power of law is so inflexible, so impersonal. We are stricken as well as lifted by it. Its comforts are not without their demands upon us. The power of the cross transcends all power of law, for it is

172

founded in the Ultimate, the heart of the Father God. It is the result of that which Paul said to be the greatest of eternal values—love.

II

This power of the cross was born in sacrifice. Jesus was not forced to undergo the rigors of Calvary. He accepted it willingly, and not as a grudging necessity. Herein is the secret of the power which the cross has been able to wield over the centuries. Men scoff at the idea of the meek inheriting the earth, and declare with vehemence that the race belongs to the strong. But when one considers history as it is written in actual deeds, such scoffing seems out of place. Experience is conclusive evidence that the man who would be strong must make himself weak. Out of such a paradox come some of the most tremendous facts of our living.

One of the rules by which humans must live is that life consists in the spending of treasures, never in the hoarding of them. Here is a miser, according to the old tales, who secretes his wealth in iron chests, and examines it only by the flickering light of a candle, when all others have retired. Lean, sallow, with talon-like hands and bilious eyes, he gloatingly allows the shining yellow metal to trickle through his bony fingers. His name stands for wealth, and within his control is vast power. But it is not really power at all, nor is he really wealthy, for by a strange obsession he can never spend it. The man who merely has money does not possess power; the man who spends it is powerful.

Here is another person who has the same miserly attitude toward his human life. He is tremulous with anxiety for his bodily safety. He guards himself assiduously from all germs; he shrinks from the weather, shivers at the rain, and constantly finds in his living suspicious symptoms of a nervous breakdown. His animal life becomes for him a hollow anxiety, so concerned is he lest it be snatched from him in some untoward moment. But that man has no power. He is a coward who dies daily, stifling every instinct for noble adventure, and allowing the lust for living to quench every opportunity for service.

Here is another who has a comfortable existence. He is neither wealthy nor miserly with that which he has. He is not unusually healthy, but is not uncomfortable about it. But he has no power in his living, for he has not learned that the secret of true power is sacrifice. He hugs to himself his material comforts, and deigns not to share them with some Lazarus whose sores are being licked by the dogs at his doorstep. No romance stirs his heart, for romance costs something, and he is not prepared to give. No love thrills his heart, for love is breathless adventure, and he is not willing to embark. He does not know that the secret of having is giving. He does not understand that the secret of enjoying is depriving oneself. He has not learned that power depends on sacrifice.

Several generations ago a young man set out to preach the gospel to the natives of Tierra del Fuego. He spent his private fortune outfitting an expedition, only to be driven back by the unfriendly inhabitants. He was a penniless, unsuccessful man, but he had not lost his power, so he placed his case before the churches. Again he was outfitted, and this time was permitted to land. One by one he watched his companions die, until at last he alone was left. The superstitious natives drove him to the shelter of his little boat. In the shadow of a torn sail he lay dying. Not one soul had been given him for his hire. Did he lack in power? Listen to his last written words as they were found in the little boat long afterward: "My little boat is a Bethel to my soul. Asleep or awake, I am happier than tongue can tell. I am starving, yet I feel neither hunger nor thirst. I feed on hidden manna and drink at the King's well. I am not disappointed, for I remember that one soweth and another reapeth." The power that Allen Gardiner had—the power of complete sacrifice—founded a church in that faraway land, and today thousands of converts water his grave with their tears.

Again, we note that the power of the cross was that of gentleness. It seems that always in religious affairs we discuss realities in paradoxical terms. Power and gentleness do not seem to be-

175

long in the same category. Yet the truth is that whosoever would have the sort of power that will make this world a place where men can live without fear, and in perfect trust of each other, must learn to be gentle with it all. Certainly the Master learned that lesson, and proclaimed it with royal accents from the outstretched arms of the Roman cross. How different, that day, was his power from the might represented by the soldiers gathered around him. Yet his power has proved its worth, while that of Rome has crumbled to dust.

Mere brute force produces a power that for the moment holds sway in human affairs. Some say that no other sort of power is understandable by men. This is the basis of the Nazi philosophy of government. Let the state be all-powerful, because the state is strong, and because opposition can be crushed by a ruthless, heartless group which happens to hold the reins of authority at the moment. It is a philosophy which has brought havoc into our world, and which has caused suffering beyond compare. But it is doomed to failure ultimately, no matter how many people it crushes at the moment. Its panzer divisions of death go only so far; then they meet the immovable law of the ages: "Whosoever would be powerful must first learn the secret of weakness."

With such sentiments most of us are in hearty agreement. But the point of these remarks lies not in the condemnation of a government far away from us, and with which none of us has a direct contact. Suppose we think of our own autocratic power-wielding. Think of your home life, where you are king or queen. Think of your office, or your schoolroom, or your factory, or whatever opportunity is yours for exerting authority. Small or big, the quality of your heart will largely determine your fitness for power. Kind treatment of others, generous service, is a measure of one's true power. To Artabazus, a courtier, Cyrus gave a golden cup. But to Chrysanthus, his favorite, he gave a kiss. Whereupon the courtier remarked, "Sire, the cup you gave me was not so good gold as the kiss you gave to Chrysanthus."

This is the sort of power worth having, and the most universally available. Not all of us will have armies at our command; not all of us will feel the thrill of power that comes to one in authority over many men. But to each of us there comes an opportunity to be powerful in our daily living. The cross is the seal that such power is not without its reward.

The final thing we note about the power of the cross is that it came from the Master's acceptance of the situation. Some conceive it to be a more excellent way to revolt against life and its consequences. They keep themselves in a continual state of rebellion against the circumstances with which they are surrounded. But these are never the people on whom the world depends.

They are like "the quarry-slave at night, scourged to his dungeon," there to nurse their lash-scarred bodies. For life has its own way of dealing with those who revolt against its demands.

Men find or lose themselves when faced with crisis! Most of us are able to live through the ordinary, and even the unusual; but when crisis comes we prove whether or not our foundations are laid upon a rock. Richard Hillary, in his graphically descriptive book *Falling Through Space*, shows us he had little power in his living until his plane was shot from under him, and he fell, a maimed and broken young man, into the North Sea. During the long months of his convalescence he found the meaning of existence, and crisis produced for him a method of life. Perhaps "Theology of Crisis" is much more significant than some of us had thought. It is magnificently real at times.

Browning, in "A Grammarian's Funeral," has an inconspicuous line, upon which the heroic in the poem really turns. He does not speak much concerning the Grammarian's early years:

Long he lived nameless: how should Spring take note
    Winter would follow?

For the Grammarian it was a careless, easy, undistinguished round of life,

Till lo, the little touch, and youth was gone!

We do not know what that "little touch" was. Perhaps in the thirties or forties a twinge of rheumatism, an unwonted flagging of the heart after exertion, a humiliating defeat of some sort, a disappointment in love—it might have been any one of a number of things. Browning, with his accustomed insight into the ways of men, simply calls it "the little touch," that made this man leave his play for work, and begin to grapple with the world. It is not different with us. Power comes to the man who has learned to meet necessities.

In our world men are casting about to discover the secret of power sufficient to meet the demands of the moment. Some, with downcast faces, see only the muck and mire of the world. They have no power, for they have no vision; and the two are inseparable. But there are others who have lifted their faces to the stars; have felt the cooling winds of the night blowing about them; have seen, as in a dream, the cross in all its shining glory "towering o'er the wrecks of time"; have heard a Voice saying confidently, "I, if I be lifted up from the earth, will draw all men unto me." Lo! these no longer wonder; they are well assured. In their hearts there is a song, and power for living flows thrillingly through their being.

THE CROSS AND THE FUTURE

Blessed be the God and Father of our Lord Jesus Christ, which according to his abundant mercy hath begotten us again unto a lively hope by the resurrection of Jesus Christ from the dead.—I Pet. 1:3

THERE IS SOMETHING INDEFINABLE ABOUT EASTER. It is comparable to Christmas, and yet is widely separated from that festival. It is woven into the life of each of us, and yet is as distinct from us as any objective event. All in all it is a puzzling affair, and yet so simply true that the wayfaring man, though a fool, understands its inherent meaning. It has put a sun in the sky for us, and opened before us vistas of triumph that are beyond the wildest imaginations of men. "Christ the Lord is risen today, Alleluia."

The story itself has been told so often that there is no virtue in merely repeating it. We have heard in song and sermon the facts of that first Easter morning, and we know full well the events that tumbled over each other in such rapid succession. It was an exciting time for those who were a part of its stupendous happenings, for nothing like this had ever taken place in the history of the world. From that day forward the currents of life flowed in new channels because of a world-shaking event.

From that day forward human affairs were different because the Son of God had set the seal of victory upon every work that he had done here upon the earth.

In a proper understanding of the Easter message of triumph there must be interwoven a proper understanding of the events that led up to this moment. We do wrong to attempt to isolate Easter as a particular incident. It is a part of the whole life of Christ, and certainly cannot be dissociated from its immediately preceding event, the cross. Without the cross Easter could not have been; without Easter the cross would not have been. God saw beyond the tragedy of Calvary, but like a dark backdrop its reality is ever present.

Consequently, in any study of the deeper meanings of the Easter celebration we do well to maintain a backward look at the cross as well as a forward look to the empty sepulcher. They are inseparable, and the one is not significant without the other. Jesus lives forever in the hearts of his people because he was willing to die upon the cross. He manifests the power of God because he was willing to renounce the power and suffer death, even the shameful death of crucifixion. Let us not lose sight of the one fact in our exuberance over the other.

It so happens that our generation is suffering the pangs of the cross. Our world has lost its way, having cast aside its maps of happiness to indulge for a season in an orgy of blood-and-thunder living. We are passing through the "glories of war" period, and among us there are many despairing hearts because of the empty hopes that surround us. Individually and collectively, we are wondering if all has been lost and the future is to be forever dark. Certainly gleams of light are not too frequent at such a time. But Easter will remind us that crosses are but forerunners of triumphs if we walk hand in hand with God.

I

Fundamentally Easter is an assurance of life. And who can honestly say that such a hope does not have its appeal? The question that stares at us from the oldest book in the world, "If a man die, shall he live again," is as modern as this morning's newspaper. Death is constantly laying its sacrilegious hands upon those whom we love, and we are continually reminded that the grim reaper is no respecter of persons, but chooseth whom he will to go with him. Such thoughts must give us pause at times, and certainly we know that hope for some further life will not be destroyed, no matter how insistently we refuse to admit its presence.

Time and again sermons have been preached upon the instinctive belief of men in the fact of immortality. This thing is forever true, and every illustration that can be adduced is one more link in an ever lengthening chain of evidence as to the truth of the Easter message. We cannot feel within our hearts that this life encompasses the possibilities of mankind. We reach out into the darkness of the future to find a hope that will prove a safe anchor for our spirits. From the aborigines of Australia, with their strange custom of removing the fingernails of a deceased person lest he dig his way out of the grave, through the most civilized customs of modern man in attending his dead, we find that the belief in future life will not be destroyed. A man may renounce it, but when the Black Camel kneels at the door of some loved one he cannot fail to feel the flutter of hope within his breast.

There is something that we can lay hold upon in such a time as this! We know the reality of the cross; we may also know the reality of the triumph which the cross foretells. We must view our religious experience as a guarantee that it is no dead King who demands our allegiance, but One who lives in the hearts of all men who will allow it to be so. Then as full light breaks over us we come to know the assurance that is granted to those who have seen in him the life and immortality for which aching hearts are searching.

Life is oftentimes a disillusioning process. We reach for some plum only to have it turn to ashes in our hands. We lay hold upon some coveted prize only to discover that its worth is illusory instead of real. We play a little, work a little, love a little, and then find that life is over and its moments of achievement have been relatively few. Each of us has a deep-seated feeling that if life could be given to us for a longer period of time we would accomplish so much more that is worth while. But the moments of existence are short, and we know that our work will be all undone when we fold our hands in the sleep that men call death. No cross of our experience is more difficult to bear than this realization.

But, as so many writers have pointed out, is not this an earnest of the life that is to be? Does not the bearing of this particular spiritual cross of frustration lead over the hill of human Calvaries to Easter itself? It is said of Beethoven that he wrote music far in advance of the day in which he lived. Indeed, it is said that some of his compositions could not be rendered correctly because the technique and instruments had not been perfected for their proper performance. So one of his biographers reminds us that it was necessary to invent new instruments and to perfect new methods of musical rendition to measure up to the genius of this master.

There is no thought more compelling or more thrilling than that of our possibilities as human beings. Our personalities may so extend themselves that we too shall be forced to live up to them, emancipating our dead selves from their lesser ambitions and earthly desires. In the understanding of the deep significance of the worth of a single personality we see quite plainly that which Jesus meant when he spoke of giving life more abundantly. The crosses of our experience become but one item along the way to glory, when we see that here and now is our opportunity to begin the proper use of life that is to go on and on through time beyond human computation. Whatever suffering may be our lot at the moment we bear with fortitude, knowing that *life* is ours and that its abundance depends entirely upon our desire to use it. The cross upon which Jesus died was but the gateway to his Father's house of many mansions—it shall not be different with those who name his name.

II

A natural corollary of the fact that Easter means life is that here is a time of joy. Into an hour of tears and pain there stole a ray of sunshine, and this ray enlarged until the whole glorious truth of his resurrection was made apparent to those friends who had been faithful to him. On black Friday Jesus died upon a cross, and the hearts of those who loved him were broken as they perceived that even this One who had unstopped the ears of the deaf, loosed the tongues of the dumb, and opened the eyes of the blind, was seemingly helpless before the brutal onslaught of Roman might. All the hopes that they had cherished concerning this Man of Nazareth were swallowed up in the night of his defeat. All the plans that had found such fertile soil

185

in their hearts were suddenly rent asunder. All the marvelous things that he had done were suddenly swept over the waterfall of the reality of his dying. These men and women were destitute, alone, and afflicted in their sorrow. It was more than the heart-shattering grief of a personal bereavement—it was the destruction of their ideals, of their ambitions, of their religious certainties. Small wonder that under the cover of the darkness that attended his dying they broke and ran like frightened sheep before an approaching thunderstorm. All the things which they believed were overturned and life was bitter in their mouths.

The events of that Friday find a startling parallel in our day. Things in which some of us believe, have been overturned; ideals by which some of us trusted that the world might be redeemed, have been tossed into the wastebasket of man's inhumanity to man; hopes for the future of mankind have been blasted and torn asunder, until there are many who are tempted to flee away beneath the darkness that surrounds us. Love is drowned by the inflowing tides of hatred; service is emasculated by the growing demands of selfishness; brotherhood is defeated by a thousand thousand rolling tanks, screaming planes, chattering guns. On every hand the darkness is thick, and the screams of men and women fighting for a crust of bread to keep the spark of life aflame mingle with the hoarse guttural accents of the dying. Ashes of defeat, of shame, of despair are spread over the heads of downtrodden people everywhere.

Into such a time the bells of Easter chime with peculiar significance to proclaim anew a message of joy. Into every sorrow-laden heart the peal of the bells enters with new meaning and new insight. Life is promising and hopeful because Easter is real and abiding. Men and women centuries ago walked in a garden where birds were singing and flowers were blooming, and they saw none of its beauties, heard none of its music, inhaled none of its perfumes, until there stood by their side the figure of One clothed in white raiment, who spake softly to them, "Be not afraid! It is I! Go and tell the others." Then were their eyes opened and they knew that victory had come and that the future was no longer sterile, but pregnant with meaning. A swelling tide of joy displaced every melancholy disposition.

No one of us can fail to be aware of the dark and dismal outlook for the tomorrows of our existence. On every hand we are constantly reminded that life is ugly and sordid, and that the future promises little more. Has not history proclaimed that we are incurably pugnacious, and that fighting and rumors of wars are the very air that we breathe? Do we not have confirmation on every hand that man glories in this thing called war, and that there is little hope of its being scourged from the councils of men? Well, perhaps, but the lines,

Two men looked through prison bars,
One saw mud, the other saw stars,

hold a remarkable lot of common sense and hope.

Let us not make Easter merely an opportunity to discuss the values of eternal life. That has its worth, and certainly Jesus came that we might reach up to such a thought and lay hold upon its deepest truth. But let us at this time of darkness remember that Easter also means the possibility of joy in the midst of pain, of light in the midst of darkness, of hope in the midst of despair. Easter is the guarantee of God that joy can triumph in the affairs of men. Jesus rose from his death couch not only to seal life for men, but also to give them that deathless happiness that comes to those who have looked upon the face of God. There are many things in the future that seem hopeless; but so long as we have the knowledge of this marvelous fact of Easter we will not despair, but will continue well assured that though the night be heavy round about us, joy cometh with the morning. "All shall yet be well," is the promise of Easter.

III

Yet again, Easter is a time of the triumph of the truth. We need terribly to be reminded of the importance of the truth in our scheme of things. Ultimately there is Something that lies at the heart of the universe that will not be downed, that cannot be hidden, that must not be ignored. To discover that Something, which men call truth, is the highest goal and function of the human race. Consciously or unconsciously each of us is engaged in such a quest. Whether we mount some prancing steed of investigation or experiment to ride far afield in search of the Holy Grail of truth, or stay on the monotonous level of everyday existence, we are all searching constantly to know more and understand more concerning the experiences through which we pass. Truth beckons us onward and we follow, slowly but relentlessly.

This does not mean that men have always been receptive to truth. The cross itself would be a denial of such a statement. Pilate, with his contemptuous sally, "What is truth?" is symbolic of many. Truth may be incarnate before a man, and he may choose to ignore it or to spurn it. Every Galileo and Copernicus and Socrates and Savonarola unites in testimony to the hesitation with which men accept truth. But that truth always wins the day is the verdict of history. We do well not to ignore its implications.

The cross one day, Easter on another—what a marvelous parable of life that simple statement becomes. It provides an insight into the future that no other event could possibly furnish. It shows us that not even death itself can prevent that which God has planned for his children. It weaves into our morbid outlook for the future a strand of color that relieves that somber blackness of the moment.

189

It sends into living the melody that so often we have dropped because of our discordant rendition of it. It reminds us again that "life can be beautiful." Truth will conquer; and no tyranny, no despot, no dictator shall ever be able to change that dynamic fact. Easter is our assurance of it.

This means that you and I must learn to link truth with the future in which we are concerned. We cannot be content to accept life as it is. There must be a vision of truth that beckons us onward and makes us dissatisfied with this world as we have found it. We do not want any "back to normal" philosophy to qualify our efforts in the world at the present time. We do not have any normal behind us—the norm is still in the future, and toward it we look. We shall destroy ourselves as a nation and as individuals if we attempt to force our world back into accustomed patterns of the past. Truth, to be effectively used, must allow for changes, for advances, for that which a modern biologist terms "emergent evolution." To lose that facility will be to stifle that which could give us breath and life. To be distraught emotionally will serve us in small stead if we use our emotions as outlets for energies that ought to be forwarding themselves into the future.

It is within the realm of our discussion to point out that any truth which is to be helpful to humankind must find itself related in an inescapable way to the future. Jesus recognized the essential worth of that as time and again he condemned the dead customs of the past that had no bearing on the life of man at its present level. His was no mere resurrection from the dead past; his was a seal on a glorious future. His was no mere returning to normal; it was an escape from the normal into the supernormal where God dwells. His vision of the Kingdom of God was not encompassed with inhibitions and prohibitions; it was a vital living dream of a world in which men had learned that brotherhood and happiness spring from hearts that are changed. He rose from the dead that he might show us the necessity of correlating truth with the future, even though that future belong to others than ourselves.

Some newspaper commentator has remarked that, although it would be sheer suicide, if Hitler should call tomorrow for an army of volunteers to invade the coasts of Britain, he would have three men offer themselves for every one that could be used. Why? Because German lads wish to die? Because they would relish leaving scarred and broken bodies along the chalky shores of England? Not at all! It is because those German boys have been so imbued with a dream of the Germany that is to be that they are willing to sacrifice whatever they have in order that truth as they see it may triumph and the world of tomorrow may be the greater Germany that they have been taught to believe is the savior of mankind.

Whatever you may say of the unmoral foundations on which their dream is founded, there is one thing that it is dangerous to say—that we can puncture that dream merely by tanks or planes or guns or men. As someone has sagely remarked, "You can't lick a dream with a question mark." Until the men of the democracies believe something strong enough to realize that our function is not to preserve the past but to create the future, we shall not likely win. Truth triumphs, but men must hold fast to it. The Easter truth was made reality because one Man believed enough to suffer through agonizing hours of a Gethsemane and a cross.

Margaret Slattery tells of a family who lost three children within a week in a diphtheria epidemic. Yet the next Easter Sunday found them in their accustomed places at the church—the mother teaching her class of girls, and the father presiding as superintendent of the Sunday school. Amid faces lined with suffering and pain that morning, these two people seemed like a benediction of peace. "How can they do it?" was the silent question asked by many a heart that day. Going home one fifteen-year-old boy said to his parents, "Mr. and Mrs. ——really believe it, don't they?" "What?" asked the father. "Oh, you know, the whole big thing about Easter." "Of course," said the father; "all Christians believe it." "Not that way!"

There's the trouble—we Christians have never believed it "that way." If we did we could change the world!

Date Due

4/14	DEC 1 '67		
4/28	NOV 9 '68		
2/9/57			
5/9	APR 14 71		
2-24	JAN 17 72		
3-10-55			
4-12-55			
DEC 4 57			
APR 13 '61			
APR 16 '63			
OCT 1 '63			
MAR 31 '64			
APR 20 '65			
DEC 28 '65			
MAY 27 '66			
June 14			
SEP 30 '66			
Oct 27			